DEAD MAN ELECTION WINS

THE ULTIMATE COLLECTION OF *OUTRAGEOUS, WEIRD, AND UNBELIEVABLE* POLITICAL TALES

PHIL MASON

sourcebooks

Published by Sourcebooks, Inc.
P.O. Box 4410, Naperville, Illinois 60567-4410
(630) 961-3900
Fax: (630) 961-2168
www.sourcebooks.com

Originally published in Great Britain in 2010 by JR Books

Library of Congress Cataloging-in-Publication Data
Mason, Phil, 1958-
  Dead man wins election : the ultimate collection of wacky and unbelievable tales from politics / Phil Mason.
  "Originally published in Great Britain in 2010 by JR Books"—t.p. verso.
  Includes index.
  (trade paper : alk. paper) 1. Politics, Practical—Humor. 2. Politics, Practical—Anecdotes. I. Title.
  PN6231.P6M37 2012
  324.02'07—dc23

2012011801

Printed and bound in United States of America.

VP 10 9 8 7 6 5 4 3 2 1

★ CONTENTS ★

*For Ally, but for whose long
(and mainly silent) suffering this volume
would not have seen the light of day.*

*In putting up with my persistent flight from
domestic life for endless days and nights, she
has perhaps approached knowing what it must
be like to be a politician's wife—a husband who
is never around when needed, who appears to be
engaged in a tedium the merits of which she
cannot begin to fathom and, worse, one which
relies on the wisdom of untold strangers whom
we'll never know for its success.*

So here's to all you strangers, too!

★ INTRODUCTION ★

In November 2000, voters from Missouri elected a dead man as their senator. Former governor Mel Carnahan had died in an air crash three weeks before election day. But he still won by a 2 percent margin. Unusual as Carnahan's achievement may sound, he is by no means unique. You will encounter seven others in these pages who have gained this ultimate accolade just in recent times, including one who won over 90 percent of the vote, and one who won on the toss of a coin. Another, although he lost, amassed over half a million votes.

You will encounter many more strange episodes within these covers, from the candidate for mayor who got his twin brother to stand in for him at a city parade that clashed with his campaign rally to the environment minister who used a stretch limo to ride to a conference to make a speech on excessive car use; from the Canadian province that found all its laws passed in 95 years to be invalid to the Australian state that discovered in 2002 that it was still officially at war with Japan; and from the legislators of West Virginia who engaged in a protracted dispute as to whether the official state musical instrument should be the fiddle or the dulcimer to the local council in Wales that kept "temporary" traffic lights in place for 28 years.

These, and hundreds more, are deeds that may redefine your view of politics, politicians, and the trade they ply on our behalf. *Dead Man Wins Election* collects the best of the worst of politicians' extraordinary antics over the past three decades (and a bit more besides). We will come across incompetence and audacity, egotism and brazenness, largesse and myopia, the mad and the bad, the feckless and the luckless: enough perhaps to make us truly wonder whether we are sane in holding on to the idea that we elect our politicians on the basis of some feeling of trust that our futures lie safe in their hands. The practice recounted here would suggest a very different story.

Politics is a rich terrain for idiosyncrasy and the unexpected. By its nature, it is a risky business. Careers rest uneasily on the periodic judgment of voters. A glittering path can be snuffed out in a single adverse turn of electoral fortune. What certainties can they look to? "All political lives…end in failure, because that is the nature of politics and of human affairs." So, in 1977, wrote British politician Enoch Powell, who is generally regarded as having crashed his own career with a single ill-judged phrase in a single speech as he summed up another exploded reputation, that of Joseph Chamberlain.

So if that is the prospect, how can we expect more from our entrusted leaders? They might be forgiven their shortcuts and their short-term outlooks. They might be forgiven their duplicities, for the chances of permanently avoiding calamity are virtually nonexistent. A frequently told Westminster story perhaps gives a clue to the essential powerlessness of a politician operating always at the mercy of "events." A cabinet minister, arriving at his new desk on the day of his appointment, finds three brown envelopes left by his predecessor, numbered one to three, with a note: "Open only when in trouble." Nine months into his job, the first crisis hits. The minister opens the first envelope. Inside is a slip that reads: "Blame your predecessor." He does, and the emergency is successfully overcome. A few months later, the next disaster hits. He opens the second envelope. The slip reads: "Reorganize your department." He does so, with a fanfare sufficient to distract attention, and he survives again. When the third calamity strikes, he turns to the third envelope, to be told: "Write out three envelopes…"

This collection will give you a completely fresh perspective on politics and its propensity for the outrageous, the extreme, and the just plain unbelievable. We will explore parliaments, the task of government, elections, the responsibilities of office and diplomacy, as well as the often unfathomable world of local and parish council politics and the mad, modern world of health and safety. We'll also portray the best and funniest political wisdom.

Most of our tales are from the last 30 years. Lest this should lend credence to any impression that political insanity is merely a modern phenomenon, we end each chapter with a selection of the choicest snippets from the pages of history to restore the balance. Politics has been the magnet for the unhinged since the dawn of civilization. That much, if little else, is clear.

What emerges from it all? Perhaps just that anything, literally anything, can be expected from our politicians. As characters they range from out-of-control egotists who excel in repelling those they come into contact with to fish-out-of-water ingenues who simply mystify us all in how or why they got involved in the first place. And there are shades at all points in between, examples of whom you are about to meet.

★ x ★

Two illustrations of these extremes serve to set the scene. For brazenness there can be no better example than the driven, and some would say power-crazy, political machine that was Lyndon Johnson. As newly appointed vice president under John F. Kennedy after an already long career on Capitol Hill, he made his mark on senators in his usual ferocious way. One day he spotted a face in a Congress corridor, shouted, "You, I've been looking for you," and pulled the unfortunate senator into his room to begin an animated pep talk about how important the legislator was to the administration. As he barreled along, he scribbled something on a piece of paper and pressed a buzzer for his secretary, who came in and took it away. Johnson kept up an unremitting torrent of political puff. A few minutes later, the secretary returned and gave the paper back to him. He glanced at it without interrupting his flow, screwed it up and threw it in the bin, and hurtled on. A journalist afterward discovered what Johnson had written on the paper: "Who is this I'm talking to?"

At the other end of the scale lie the likes of Ernest Bevin. We see in chapter 7 how this former trade union leader and genial embodiment of the working class, whom Attlee remarkably made foreign secretary in the postwar labor government of 1945–51, defused ambassadorial pomposity with his common touch. Shortly after taking up his post at the Foreign Office, Bevin returned to his office on a Friday afternoon to find that his private secretary had left on his desk a huge pile of papers, on top of which was a carefully penned note: "The Secretary of State may care to peruse these at his leisure before Monday." Without looking at his homework, Bevin penned an equally short and obliging note and left for the weekend: "A kindly thought, but erroneous."

He perhaps also epitomizes the gap that ofttimes exists between politics as the personal endeavor and politics as "the system," the machine that controls. It is this gap, and a politician's success or failure (and desire) in bridging it, that makes politics such a rich territory for oddity, and the terrain that we explore here.

Dead Man Wins Election ought to sow doubt in your minds about anyone standing for political office. When you reach the end, you too may conclude we Americans, who like to think of ourselves as the world's fullest exponents of the democratic creed, were perhaps saying more than we knew when we chose as our national motto, "In God we trust." For as sure as anything, we have been taking a risk with our earthly rulers ever since.

Phil Mason

THE BEAST WITHIN:
OFFICEHOLDERS

When Harold Macmillan became prime minister in 1957, his appointment took second place on the front page of his local paper in Sussex, beaten by a report of a Brighton and Hove Albion football match. He kept the cutting on his desk at No. 10 in order, he said, to guard against the temptation toward self-importance. Most politicians are not like Macmillan. As they seek to climb the greasy pole, the animal inside is all too often revealed in bizarre ways.

QUESTIONABLE CHARACTERS

Julian Castro, campaigning to become mayor of San Antonio, Texas, in 2005, threw away his chances when he dealt with a clash of schedules by getting his identical twin brother to stand in for him at a civic parade while he attended a campaign meeting. Leading in the opinion polls at the time, he had brother Joaquin, a state legislator, walk in the city's high-profile annual River Parade, waving to the crowds, while he attended his meeting. Claiming afterward that he had never intended to deceive, and blaming a parade announcer for misidentifying his brother as himself, Castro failed to survive the controversy. It did not help that the brothers previously had similar incidents, Julian having been accused of impersonating his brother when Joaquin ran for his state legislator seat.

Julian lost the election 51 percent to 49. "I don't think he was ready to become mayor," said his victorious opponent, diplomatically. He bounced back, however, and eventually won the mayoralty in 2009.

A CANADIAN POLITICIAN FROM the national House of Commons received criticism in January 2001 for his own bizarre attempt to deceive. Rahim Jaffer, MP for Edmonton and chairman of the Opposition Canadian Alliance Party's small business committee, was impersonated by his assistant for nearly an hour for a radio interview after a diary mix-up meant that Jaffer was unavailable for the talk show. The station, tipped off by suspicious listeners, contacted Jaffer afterward to confirm it had been him. He initially maintained that he had done the interview, before later confessing that his aide had fulfilled the commitment. By way of contrition, he told listeners that his assistant had resigned. Although his party suspended him for several months, he hung on to his seat until losing it in the 2008 election.

PAUL REITSMA, A LIBERAL Party member of the British Columbia legislative assembly in Canada, appeared to enjoy wide support among his Vancouver Island constituents if the local papers were anything to go by. They were always carrying letters to the editor from the community praising his performance. Reitsma's world collapsed in 1998 when one of the local organs used handwriting comparisons to show that he had been writing them himself. He confessed to being responsible for penning dozens of self-praising letters over a 10-year period, sending them under fictitious names to laud his own work and cast aspersions on his opponents. He was promptly expelled from the party, although he refused to resign his seat. Over 25,000 outraged local voters signed a petition for his dismissal under a new provincial recall procedure. After hanging on for two months, he resigned, shortly before he would have become the first Canadian politician to be forcibly removed from office by the procedure.

BOURNEMOUTH LOCAL COUNCILOR BEN Grower was unmasked in 2009 as having submitted Internet postings under a disguised identity to praise his own performance. As he was one of only a handful of Labor members on the 54-seat council, generating publicity evidently required extra help. He turned to leaving laudatory comments on the website of his local newspaper, the *Daily Echo*, under several pseudonyms, extolling the contribution he was making to services. Examples of his comments were published by the paper when it traced the posts back to an address owned by Grower. He left comments like, "At least two councilors seem to be concerned about this mess. Well done Cllrs. Ratcliffe and Grower," and "Just shows that the area does have councilors who care about their residents. Well done Ted Taylor, Ben Grower, and Beryl Baxter." Another purported to come from a detached observer: "I have friends who live in the area. They say councilors Ted Taylor and Ben Grower fought hard against the proposals." Initially denying the claims, Grower eventually acknowledged the ruse, saying that other councilors were doing the same to get their names in the media.

GLOUCESTER LIBERAL DEMOCRAT COUNCILOR Jeremy Hilton, trying to whip up support for his campaign to become the local MP, was caught in March 2010 trying to write his own fan mail. He was caught emailing scripts of letters to others, asking them to "cut and paste" them into letters, which they would send to the county's newspaper under their own names. They would proclaim him as the best man for representing the city at the coming general election. The ruse only came to light in a way that questioned his organizational attributes for the role he aspired to—he mistakenly fired off the obsequious email to the newspaper itself. More woe followed at the May election—he came in a distant third.

THE 500-ODD RESIDENTS OF the small Maryland community of Friendsville (motto: "the friendliest little town in Maryland") have lived up to their name by reelecting their mayor, Spencer Schlosnagle, 13 times in succession from 1986 despite his wayward record in public decorum. He has been convicted on three separate occasions, in 1992, 1993, and 1995, for exposing himself in public. For the 1993 offense, he had to undertake 30 days' community work, returning to jail each night. Then, in 2004, he was fined $100 for leading police on a car chase when being apprehended for speeding. His political standing, however, did not seem to suffer. He still went on to win reelection in 2006, and at the time of writing is still mayor, up for election again in February 2012.

ILLINOIS ASSEMBLYMAN ROGER MCAULIFFE, a former police-man, successfully introduced legislation in 1995 that enabled all former police officers who went on to serve in the state assembly to be eligible to draw pensions from both the police and the legislature. At the time of its introduction, the measure benefited precisely one person—himself. There may have been divine justice, however. The following year, McAuliffe drowned in a boating accident. He was a day short of his 58th birthday, and never got to draw on the benefits he had craftily created.

THE NEW ZEALAND PRIME minister Helen Clark was discovered in 2002 to have signed a painting done by an unknown artist as her own work for a charity auction. The piece, described as "a splashy abstract landscape," had been done three years earlier when Clark was leader of the Opposition for an animal welfare charity who had sought daubings from celebrity figures. A staff member had quietly commissioned an obscure artist, Lauren Fouhey, to do one for her. Clark then signed both the front and the back of the picture, and it successfully earned $1,000 at the event. "I was trying to be helpful when I didn't have the time," she explained when the disgruntled businessman who had bought the picture as a potential investment found out the truth. Adding to her embarrassment, Clark was by then also minister for Arts and Culture, a post she had awarded herself days after winning office in 1999, saying that her personal pet project was furthering the arts. Although fraud offenses carried a punishment of up to 10 years in jail, police authorities decided after looking into the case for three months that a prosecution was "not in the public interest."

IMAGE PROBLEMS

Former president Bill Clinton, who portrayed his presidency as the watershed period for the modern "Information Age," was revealed after he left office to have been a little less of a pioneer than he purported to be. In 1998, for example, in a speech to the Massachusetts Institute of Technology, he lauded how the information-tion technology that had been harnessed and promoted by his administration had been responsible for more than a third  of America's economic expansion and confidently gushed how "all students should feel as comfortable with a keyboard as a chalkboard, as comfortable with a laptop as a textbook." Three years after his departure from the White House, staff at his presidential library archiving the president's records disclosed that of the 40 million or so emails that his office had produced, Clinton himself had sent just…two. One of these did not officially qualify as it was a test message to check that he knew where the "send" button was. In actuality, it appeared that he only sent one real message—to orbiting astronauts in a publicity stunt. Skip Rutherford, the library's president, commented, seemingly unnecessarily, that Clinton was "not a techno-klutz."

MITT ROMNEY, FORMER MASSACHUSETTS governor, got off to a rocky start on his 2008 presidential campaign as he tried to establish a profile for himself as a man of the common people. Declaring himself in April 2007 to have been a hunter "pretty much all my life," it later transpired that this amounted to going hunting twice—once when he was 15 years old and not again until the previous year. He dropped out of the race within a month of the first primary votes in early 2008.

AS THE 2000 U.S. presidential election approached, former vice president Al Gore established his future campaign credentials around concern for the environment. Even before the campaign officially opened, observers noted his visits to key states had taken on a suspiciously election-style feel. In July 1999, he went to New Hampshire, which happened to hold the crucial first primary election. His aides suggested he do a press call paddling a canoe on the picturesque waters of the Connecticut River that runs through the state. It later emerged that U.S. Secret Service agents had insisted the local authorities release four billion gallons of water from an upriver dam to ensure that the VP's canoe did not get stuck on the riverbed. Water was at unprecedented low levels, as the whole of New England was suffering its worst ever drought. By the time Gore performed his sail-past in front of the assembled press corps, the Connecticut was 10 inches higher, ensuring a safe passage. Within minutes of his departure, the water was shut off and the river sank back to a trickle.

ISRAELI NEWSPAPERS HAD A field day in February 2007 when Defense Minister Amir Peretz, who had been widely criticized since his appointment the previous year for his lack of military background, was photographed looking through binoculars with the lens caps still on. Of particular hilarity was the fact that he raised the glasses to his eyes three times, nodding in acknowledgement each time as the chief of staff drew his attention to objects on the horizon, giving no apparent sign he was having difficulty seeing what his guide was pointing out. He quit the post four months later.

DURING A RECORD DROUGHT in Victoria, Australia, in 1982, the state premier hosted a morale-boosting press visit to the worst-affected farms. As the media set up in the middle of a remote, parched field for a press conference to be carried live on early evening news, almost on cue a dramatic rainstorm broke. The premier persevered, and the scene was captured for posterity of 30 politicians and local dignitaries bemoaning the effects of the drought—in the middle of a muddy field huddled under umbrellas and the odd sodden newspaper.

MISTAKES THAT REVEAL

Irked by a political opponent who had called him a liar, California Governor Arnold Schwarzenegger succumbed to temptation in October 2009 when he wrote back to the lawmaker vetoing his proposed legislation. Encoded in the official-looking response to San Francisco Democrat Tom Ammiano was an obscene message. Reading vertically downward, the first letter of each line spelled out "fuck you." Officially, Schwarzenegger's press spokesperson was "surprised" at the "strange coincidence."

A MORALE-BOOSTING COMMUNICATIONS DRIVE by Britain's Labor Party headquarters to help MPs keep up-to-date with the leadership backfired in early 2005 when some members failed to read the material fully before dispatching thousands of copies of a self-promoting letter around their constituencies. Draft pro forma letters containing a fulsome account of the government's achievements were sent to all MPs, littered with uplifting sentiments such as "And nowhere can we be more proud than here in." with helpful markers indicating "(insert constituency name here)." Unfortunately, at least nine MPs simply cut and pasted the text unamended onto their own letterhead and sent them on their way.

DOING IT MY WAY

Harold Gunn, campaigning as a Republican candidate for the Texas House of Representatives in 2000, lost at the primary stage in March when it emerged that he had written and appeared in a pornographic film featuring naked women jogging through a Houston park and lathering themselves with motor oil. Gunn said this showed him to be "a communicator," adding, "It's as tasteful as it can get with naked women in it." He was trounced by his opponent 78 percent to 22.

IN A SIMILAR VEIN, Teres Kirpikli, a female member of Sweden's conservative Christian Democrat Party, campaigned in the country's 2002 parliamentary elections on the platform that pornography should be broadcast on national television throughout Saturdays to encourage more people to have sex to help boost the country's population, "l want erotica and porn on television every Saturday and all day," she said, adding, "l think most people like porn, even though they don't want to admit it." She was quickly dropped by her party leadership.

VICENTE SANZ, A MEMBER of the Spanish center-right Popular Party in the regional assembly of Valencia, was sacked by his party in June 1994 for his honesty. He had said in an interview that he was in politics "to line my pockets."

THOMAS KRÜGER CAMPAIGNED AS Social Democrat candidate for Berlin in the German federal elections in 1994 by plastering the city with posters of himself in the nude, accompanied by the slogan: "An honest politician with nothing to hide."

THE MAYOR OF GUAYAQUIL, Ecuador's biggest city, responded to local journalists' harassing style at press conferences in 2003 by hiring a parrot to speak for him. Jaime Nebot, who had been rankled by the press corps' criticisms of his policies, introduced the bird saying, "Some people only approach me with nonsense talk, so the parrot will answer back in the same way. I need to use my time to work."

THREE WEEKS AFTER SHE won election to Maidstone Borough Council in May 2003, Annabelle Blackmore announced she was leaving Kent to accompany her financial consultant husband, who had been posted to Bermuda for two years. She rejected suggestions that she should resign as councilor, maintaining she could "do an OK job" representing her constituents in the village of Marden just as effectively from the island, 3,500 miles away. "If I resigned, I feel I would be relinquishing my responsibility and letting down those who voted for me." Blackmore survived a complaint to the English Standards Board, which oversees conduct of elected officials. It found that she had not brought her office or council into disrepute, or broken any code of conduct. She appears to have completed the long-distance service adequately enough to continue to be reelected to the council where, by 2009 and back in Marden, she had become chair of the Environment and Leisure Committee. According to the council's log of meeting attendances, it was September 2007, four and a half years after her election, before she actually attended her first meeting.

THE MAYORS OF TWO Paris suburbs engaged in a skirmish on traffic congestion in 2009 by declaring the same stretch of road a one-way street, but in opposite directions. Patrick Balkany, conservative mayor of Levallois-Perret, decided to improve flows in his area by designating a main road as a one-way route. His neighbor, socialist mayor of Clichy-la-Garenne, Gilles Catoire, complained that the decision increased congestion in his area and declared the stretch of the road under his control one-way, but in the other direction. The stalemate was referred up the lengthy administrative chain to the prefect of Paris for a ruling. Balkany eventually won out.

NO EXCUSES

Philadelphia city councilor Angel Ortiz was discovered in 2001 to have been driving for the last 25 years without a license, including 17 years when he was a municipal employee or council member. "I kept trying to make time to get a new license," he claimed, "but it seemed that something pressing always took precedence." When police delved further, they found he also had 53 outstanding parking tickets.

WHILE CHAIRMAN OF A 1982 New Zealand parliamentary committee examining a toughening of the country's drunk driving laws, junior minister of Trade and Industry Keith Allen was convicted and fined NZ$145—for drunk driving.

LIBERAL POLITICIAN BARONESS SEEAR failed to fulfill her engagement as a guest speaker at a British Institute of Management conference in 1979. A spokesperson tactfully put it down to "an unfortunate slip in transport." The conference was entitled "Can Women Manage?"

DATUK LEO MOGGIE, MALAYSIA'S telecommunications minister, laid on an elaborate publicity event in 1986 to herald the country's advances in telephone technology and mark the signing up of the millionth subscriber. In front of the press corps, he dialed the lucky customer—and got a wrong number.

THE LEADER OF THE Swedish Conservative Party, Ulf Adelsohn, was charged with illegally importing a cordless telephone in 1985. His claim not to know it was against the law rang a little hollow. The act banning such phones had been passed and signed by him when communications minister.

BRITISH ENVIRONMENT MINISTER ALAN Meale attended a conference in Peterborough in April 1999 to press the government's green credentials and speak about the environmental damage caused by excessive car travel. He turned up at the venue having been driven the two miles from the railway station in a stretch limo that did 17 miles to the gallon. Meale was soon lecturing the audience that "the way we travel is damaging our towns, harming our countryside and already changing the climate of the planet."

LABOR DEPUTY PRIME MINISTER John Prescott got into the same hot water at the party conference in Bournemouth that September by using a three-car convoy to take him and wife Pauline the 300 yards from their hotel to the conference hall. He was due to deliver a speech on increasing the use of public transportation. He initially, and in the media's eyes unchivalrously, blamed the journey on his wife's dislike of having her hair blown around by the sea breeze. He then cited security. The next day, he walked.

FRENCH CAR MAGAZINE *AUTO Plus* in October 2003 caught two French ministers speeding on their way to the official inauguration ceremony of the country's first speed cameras. Transportation minister Gilles de Robien was clocked by a journalist's radar gun going 61 miles per hour in the suburbs of Paris where the limit was 43 miles per hour. Future president Nicolas Sarkozy, then interior minister, sped past at 64 miles per hour. De Robien's office later did not contest the evidence, explaining that the minister was running late and had to be present, as he was presiding at the ceremony. In contrast, and perhaps indicative of his future trajectory, Sarkozy yielded no ground, getting his spokesperson to tell the media that they were "verifying the conditions under which the speeds were recorded."

TWO YEARS AFTER ITS creation, Argentina's Ethics Office, established to set standards for integrity and honesty in government, was voted by a survey of electors as one of the most corrupt institutions in the country. Of 40 public institutions covered in the poll, the graft-busting office was seen as the fourth most corrupt body, after the country's trade unions, customs service, and the judicial system.

IGNORANCE IN MOTION

A satirical magazine in Washington, DC, shed an alarming light on the lack of worldly knowledge of newly elected members of the 1993 Congress. During apparently serious interviews, the reporter threw in a question about an entirely nonexistent country. To the question, "What should we be doing about the ethnic cleansing in Freedonia?" a large number of politicians rolled out very serious answers. Corrine Brown, a freshly elected Florida member, called the situation "very, very sad," adding, "We need to take action to assist the people." James Talent (Missouri) opined, "Anything we can do to use the good offices of the U.S. government to assist stopping the killing over there, we should do." Jay Dickey from Arkansas took the easy route and blamed then-president Clinton for the debacle. Jay Inslee, a Washington State representative, confessed not to be familiar with Freedonia, but urged action nevertheless as, "It's coming to the point now that turning a blind eye to it for the next ten years is not the answer." Steve Buyer (Indiana) acknowledged, "It's a different situation than the Middle East." The magazine commented that politicians "are asked a lot of dumb questions, and they are all used to supplying answers."

IN MARCH 1993, BUCHAREST television conducted a similar survey of Romania's legislators. Reporters asked several members for their reactions to the high levels of hydrogen being found in drinking water. Most expressed themselves appalled and concerned. An Opposition spokesperson described the "problem" as "yet another proof of the government's incompetence."

In September 2007, a New Zealand MP fell for a long-running hoax exposing the gullibility of MPs who jump on political bandwagons. She wrote to the country's health department demanding immediate action to curb use of the drug dihydrogen monoxide. Jacqui Dean, Opposition National Party member for Otago, urged health minister Jim Anderton, in charge of government drug policy, to have his advisory committee on drugs take a view. He wrote back pointing out that the substance was...water.

Italian politician Tommaso Coletti provoked fury in 2006 when he used the infamous Auschwitz slogan "Work makes you free" to promote local job centers in his area. The president of Chieti province in the south of the country, Coletti wrote, "I don't remember where I read this phrase but it was one of those quotes that have an instant impact on you because they tell an immense truth." His regional governor quickly apologized to the local Jewish community.

When the House of Commons editors of *Hansard*, the daily verbatim record of parliamentary debates, analyzed a week's worth of proceedings in July 1989 to discover what size of dictionary base they needed for new computerized shorthand machines, they discovered that MPs used only 12,000 words. The average vocabulary of an educated native English speaker is estimated to be about 24,000 to 30,000.

DESPERATE MEASURES

In September 1994 Japhet Ekidor, assistant minister for Lands and Settlement in the Kenyan government, bit off the ear of a political rival in a brawl during a public meeting in the rural district of Turkana. The pair was locked in a dispute over who should be the head of a local charity. Ekidor severed the ear of Danson Ekuam, the local MP, after Ekuam had bitten him on the arm. Despite calls for the minister's dismissal for embarrassing the government, it was the MP who ended up being charged with assault.

FRENCH TOURISM MINISTER OLIVIER Stirn resigned in disgrace in July 1990 after he used a novel way to ensure a high-profile policy summit he was organizing was a successful event in the eyes of the media. The three-day Dialogue 2000, a centerpiece of the socialist government's program, attracted a stream of government ministers on the first morning, but the audience dwindled dramatically in the afternoon. With two days still to go, and thinking to spare blushes, Stirn's aides hastily contacted an employment agency and secured 200 out-of-work actors to fill the seats. For the rest of the conference, the press witnessed a rapturous and intense audience hanging on every word of the party spokesmen. The ruse was only discovered at the end when a departing journalist was mistakenly handed an envelope with the agreed day's fee.

LORD PALMERSTON HOLDS THE all-time record in British politics for ministerial service --48 years, including war secretary for an unbroken 18 years, three times as foreign secretary (16 years), once as home secretary (2 years) and twice as prime minister (over 9 years). He combined unparalleled energy for work with a fearsome temper that was always on the point of boiling over into a rupture with his cabinet colleagues. He was renowned for regularly threatening to leave the government by firing off a resignation letter to the prime minister of the day. His preferred method of delivery was to employ a lame war veteran as messenger, who would be dispatched across the quadrangle of the Ministry toward Downing Street and the PM's office. Invariably, Palmerston's temper cooled nearly as soon as the messenger had left, so he retained the services of a second (able-bodied) valet, among whose duties it was to head off in pursuit of the first man and overtake the slow-moving letter-bearer before he had chance to leave the precincts.

ODD IDEAS

Instead of concentrating on his constituents' more worldly concerns, maverick Nebraska state senator Ernie Chambers embarked on a quixotic mission in September 2007 to sue God. Claiming he was doing so to reinforce the right under the U.S. Constitution to bring any issue to court, however frivolous, Chambers lodged a claim in the state courts seeking an injunction preventing God—whom he cited as causing "calamitous catastrophes resulting in the widespread death, destruction, and terrorization of millions upon millions of Earth's inhabitants"—from inflicting further "grave harm" to his constituents. He lost the first hearing in the district court and his appeal was thrown out a year later on a technicality—that God, not having an address, could not be served papers to be notified of the proceedings as required by the Constitution. Chambers announced that he disagreed with the ruling on the grounds that since the court acknowledged God's existence, and hence His omniscience, "as God knows everything, God has notice of this lawsuit." However, by the time the verdict came, Chambers had had to retire from the Senate in compliance with term-limits laws Nebraskans had—they might now think wisely introduced a few years earlier.

THE ULTIMATE INSULT

It is one thing not to be recognized by the common people; another when it is one's own staff. Hungary's new defense minister, Janos Szabo, suffered that indignity in 1998 when he arrived to preside over an officers' inauguration ceremony. Guards on the gate of the army base refused to allow him in, as no one recognized him. Szabo later issued photographs of himself to every military base in the country, with orders to put them up at gates and in duty officers' rooms.

A SURVEY BY *PARIS MATCH* magazine in 1991 discovered that more than 8 of out 10 French people could not spell the name of their leader, François Mitterrand, almost 10 years into his presidency.

 PERHAPS THE MOST HUMBLING discovery for the egocentric politician is the realization that people do not take much notice of them. A 1982 experiment by West Germany's reputable Emnid Institute tested the knowledge of the electorate with spectacular results. Asking respondents to rank the popularity of a list of current cabinet ministers, an entirely fictitious minister whom the survey had invented for the exercise came in sixth. "Minister Meyers" beat a number of German heavyweights, including the ministers of both defense and the interior.

FROM THE HISTORY BOOKS

The most durable elected politician of all time is believed to be József Madarász, who has the longest span of service, spanning 83 years. He was a member of the Hungarian Parliament, initially between 1832 and 1836 and again between 1848 and 1850, but then continuously after 1861 until his death in 1915.

THE LONGEST CONTINUOUSLY SERVING elected national politician is believed to be Charles Pelham Villiers, who sat in the British House of Commons for 63 years and 6 days until his death in January 1898, aged 96.

CONSERVATIVE MEMBER CHRISTOPHER SYKES represented three Yorkshire constituencies in his 27-year parliamentary career dating from 1865 to 1892. In all that time, he spoke only 6 times and asked 3 questions.

GEORGES CLEMENCEAU, ONE OF France's greatest politicians, who had a 40-year career in Parliament and served twice as prime minister—between 1906 and 1909 and again during the crisis of the First World War—was paranoid about being caught unprepared. He took to the habit over decades of sleeping fully dressed, replete with shoes and sometimes even gloves. On waking each morning, he would promptly change.

THE MARQUESS OF SALISBURY was so unconcerned about his appearance that when he was in Monaco recovering from illness in the summer of 1886, he was turned away from the casino at Monte Carlo for being too scruffy. He had just ceased being prime minister at the time.

WITH SHADES OF MODERN PR concerns, Italian dictator Mussolini compensated for his short stature by standing on hidden stools to make speeches and sitting in a specially created higher chair at meetings to bring him up to the same level as others. Photographers were strictly forbidden from disclosing the aids. When first in power, he had taken to wearing a bowler hat, until his advisors told him that the Anglo-Saxon press was remarking on the image's similarities with "the fat one" of the comic duo Laurel and Hardy.

IN SEPTEMBER 1942, AS the tide of the Second World War turned against the Fascist powers in Europe, with Italian troops facing acute shortages of ammunition, uniforms, and supplies, and the country 10 months away from being invaded by the Allies, Mussolini approved the expenditure of several million pounds to improve the winter sports facilities at Cortina, in the hope that he might win the right to host the first postwar Winter Olympics.

BEING THE VANGUARD OF the Marxist revolution, champion of workers' power and proponent of social equality did not stop Lenin from accumulating nine Rolls-Royces. According to the company, Lenin ordered and received a unique model—one fitted with tank-like tracks at the rear and skis at the front, which allowed him to get about in the frozen Russian winters. The explanation given at the time, that he was simply using vehicles that had been requisitioned from the czar, was entirely untrue. Lenin employed a buyer in London to purchase all his cars new.

2

TRIALS AND ERRORS: ELECTIONS

The democratic process requires regular elections. Attention usually focuses on judging the extent to which they are free and fair. Our interest here lies a step or two beyond the norm. Even in free and fair contests, the startlingly unusual is more common than you would think. An election is the warlike moment when the human ambition for elected office is forced to place itself at the mercy of the vagaries of the common people, all armed with their fragment of the decision—their vote. How those two forces play off each other is the subject of this chapter. We must begin, however, where any review of electoral oddity must start—with the bizarre lengths to which autocrats have gone to mangle the process in order to show outwardly that they are playing the democratic game.

FREE AND FAIR?

As the West mobilized itself for invasion in the autumn of 2002, Iraq's Saddam Hussein held a referendum on his leadership. On October 15, in an atmosphere of hysteria across the country, 11 million voters were encouraged to exceed the vote of support they had given him in the last plebiscite seven years earlier when 99.96 percent approved of him continuing in office.

Amid the nationalist fervor being whipped up by the impending hostilities with the West, there were few observances of normal electoral niceties. The absence of polling booths—voters marked their ballots openly in front of the watchful eyes of the security forces—was portrayed by state media as symbolic of the transparency of the vote. Other regulations appeared relaxed. A British journalist witnessed a six-year-old boy cast his vote in Saddam's home town of Tikrit "amid much acclaim."

When the government announced the result later the next day, Vice President Izzat Ibrahim declared that every single one of the 11,445,638 Iraqis on the electoral roll had cast their vote, and every single one had voted in favor of Saddam Hussein's continued rule.

Observers noted that the victory was the first unanimous vote in electoral history. North Korea's Kim Il-sung had claimed a 100 percent vote in 1962, but even he had not claimed a 100 percent turnout. Ibrahim told Western reporters the referendum "was a unique manifestation of democracy...superior to all other forms of democracy, even [that of] countries which are besieging Iraq and trying to suffocate it."

SIMILAR PROBLEMS AFFLICTED PHILIPPINES President Ferdinand Marcos's last election in February 1986. Reports before polling day indicated massive fraud in the registration of voters. One small suburban house in the capital, Manila, was recorded as having 204 people living in it. Observers mused on the apparent overcrowding, suggesting that some ought to move next door where only 147 appeared to live. A remote jungle town returned a voting list that was two and a half times the size of its last known population. Not surprisingly, Marcos officially won the election, but the corruption was so transparent that even he was forced to admit "irregularities." He left the country within a week of the results for exile in the United States.

THE GREATEST EFFORT TO try to look proper was made by communist Albania. In its 1982 general election, official results claimed that every one of the country's 1,627,968 eligible voters had cast their ballots. Support for the ruling regime was not universal, however. A spokesperson told news agencies that eight ballots were found invalid and one elector voted against.

Things had clearly improved five years later. The official returns for the February 1987 election showed that only one invalid vote had been counted out of more than 1.8 million ballots. There were no negative votes.

EXAGGERATING THE LEVEL OF support at political rallies during election campaigns is a tried-and-tested tactic. When the Mexican National Action Party claimed a turnout of 100,000 for a rally in the national elections in 1988, an opposition newspaper contested the estimate, reporting that barely 20,000 had taken part. To prove his point, the editor of *El Norte* blew up a photograph of the rally and, under the watchful eye of a lawyer, got his staff to stick a pin into the head of every attendee. At the end of the exercise, the issue was resolved with 11,153 pins. The paper published its result the following day—adding to the effect by sarcastically presenting the findings as being a correction to its own original overestimate.

THE DEAD ARE RETURNED

State senator John Wilson was reelected in Austin, Texas, in 1982 despite having died 44 days before polling day. He won 66 percent of the vote.

POPULAR PATSY MINK WON her seat for the 14th consecutive time in the House of Representatives in Hawaii in 2002, even though she had died five weeks before the election. She won an impressive 56 percent of the vote against three other candidates.

 THE PRESTIGIOUS *NEW YORK Times* urged voters in primary elections for Congress in 1992 to vote for a dead candidate. Ted Weiss, a long-serving Democratic politician in Manhattan's West Side, had died the day before the poll. The paper urged the electorate not to allow that to let in his only opponent, a right-wing extremist. The locals dutifully and overwhelmingly did so, giving the dead man 54,168 votes to his rival's measly 7,560.

HARRY STONEBRAKER WAS REELECTED for his fourth term as mayor of the small community of Winfield, Missouri, in April 2009, having died a month before polling day. Astonishingly, he won by a landslide with 90 percent of the vote.

Carl Geary was elected mayor of Tracy City, a community of 1,600 near Chattanooga, Tennessee, in April 2010, having died of a heart attack at the start of the campaign. He trounced his only rival, winning over three-quarters of the vote. Barbara Brock, who had campaigned on a platform of beautifying the city, showed less than fulsome grace in defeat, bewailing the fact that the council would be run by someone "pushing up the daisies instead of planting them." A local restaurateur offered a confirmatory insight into the electorate's view of her: "I knew he was deceased, but we wanted someone other than her."

Such events do not just happen for minor office in out-of-the-way places. Even at a national level, dead candidates can succeed. In the 2000 national election, former Missouri governor Mel Carnahan won his campaign to sit in the U.S. Senate for his state despite having been killed in an air crash three weeks before election day. He won by a 2 percent margin. His wife temporarily took the seat, before losing a year later.

Sherman Block secured more than a third of the vote in the election for Los Angeles County sheriff in 1998 even though he had died five days before polling day. He had held the post for 17 years and had been expected to win again comfortably, despite his chronic illness that required him to undergo dialysis three times a week. He even managed to vote for himself by sending in a postal ballot before his death. Block supporters continued his campaign despite his death in the closing days of the election, reasoning that if the dead man was elected the Sheriff Office's Board of Supervisors would have to chose the new sheriff rather than the post going to his opponent. An incredible 629,289 Los Angeles residents turned out to vote for the dead candidate, Block winning 39 percent of the poll.

I WANT TO BE ELECTED

Ilona Staller, a 35-year-old Hungarian-born porn actress, made headlines in Italy's 1987 general election when

she was elected as a Radical Party MP. She became notorious for stripping in public, once leading a demonstration topless to persuade sailors about to be dispatched on a controversial NATO mission to the Arabian Gulf to mutiny and make love instead. One account sonorously described her election campaign: "Her main argument has been to take off her clothes and occasionally to let voters fondle her breasts. This seems to have restored the Italian faith in politics, and gained her a respectable number of votes."

After her election success, she became an active member of the Defense Committee, but missed a crucial debate on the Gulf deployment because she was making a pornographic film. She also offered to have sex with Saddam Hussein in 1991 if he agreed to release Western hostages he was holding as Allied forces readied for the Gulf War. "I would do it holding my nose and closing my eyes," she said, "but I would do it for peace." She completed a full term and retired from politics in 1992. She attempted a revival in 2002 when she stood for mayor in the northern town of Monza, but won only 1.5 percent of the vote.

SILVIO BERLUSCONI, ITALY'S PRIME minister from 2001 to 2006 and 2008 to 2011, became a byword for scandal and sexual sleaze. The long-standing national passion for turning elections into beauty contests reached its apogee under the septuagenarian leader. Forming his government on retaking power in 2008, he attracted publicity for appointing Mara Carfagna, a former topless model, as his minister for equal opportunities. She quickly became dubbed "the world's sexiest minister." For the 2009 elections to the European Parliament, he nominated a bevy of attractive young women as candidates for his center-right People of Freedom Party. They included a TV meteorologist and nightclub hostess and an actress, but his plans were scotched when Berlusconi's long-suffering wife publicly derided them as "shameless trash for the entertainment of the emperor."

A year later, with Berlusconi separated and facing divorce proceedings amid a prostitute scandal, the showgirls resurfaced as candidates for the party's regional election campaign in March 2010. By then he had added Nicole Minetti, a 25-year-old dental hygienist whom he had met when having his teeth repaired after an assault during a rally, Graziana Capone, a sultry model nicknamed the "Angelina Jolie of Puglia," and Francesca Provetti, a Miss Italy finalist. Despite the controversies, Berlusconi's party surprised pundits by improving its standings on polling day.

FINNISH MP JYRKI KASVI, campaigning for reelection for the Green League in 2007, translated his website into Klingon, the fictional *Star Trek* language, apparently as a means of showing his connections to the interests of young people. He successfully retained his seat.

WHEN A CONTROVERSIAL HYPNOTIST and faith healer, Anatoly Kashpirovsky, who had become a national sensation for his televised mass-healing events, stood in Russia's December

1993 election, he was forbidden by officials from canvassing in his constituency for fear he would use his powers to unduly influence electors. He had to run his campaign entirely from abroad. He based himself in the United States and, astonishingly, won. He sat in Parliament for two years until leaving permanently for America in 1995.

Taiwanese elections have acquired a reputation for wackiness and unorthodox campaign methods since repressive one-party government ended on the island in 1987. Chen Shui-bian, the opposition victor in the 2000 presidential election, used his nationwide chain of clothes stores to promote his image during the campaign. Every item he sold bore his nickname. He also sold small plastic dolls of himself dressed in a range of characters. The most popular were said to be Chen dressed as a long-haired, bandana-wearing Rambo muscleman and as a punk rocker with spiky green hair.

The trend had been set by the ruling party, which in local polls the previous year had dressed 75-year-old President Lee Teng-hui in various outfits as he campaigned around the country. At one rally he appeared in a *Star Trek* uniform; at others as King Arthur, a tribal chieftain, and a farmer, complete with live water buffaloes.

In 1992, the newly founded Labor Party tried to win hearts and minds by employing the talents of Hsu Hsiao-tan, a 30-year-old nude model, for the seat in the southern city of Kaoshiung. Her talents were bountifully expressed. Cited in an academic review of political development in Taiwan as "a rather unorthodox strategy," Hsu spent most of her campaign baring her breasts, jumping naked into polluted rivers, and streaking through municipal rubbish dumps. "My body is a political weapon. My breasts are nuclear warheads," she declared. She amassed over 32,000 votes and fell only 108 short of getting elected.

THE BEER LOVERS' PARTY won nearly 3 percent of the vote in the Polish general election of 1991, and captured 16 seats in the 460-seat national Parliament. They remained there until the 1993 elections, when they all lost their seats.

IN 1994, DANES ELECTED Jacob Haugaard, a comedian styling himself the head of the Union of Conscientiously Work-Shy Elements. Although his campaign pledges included promises of better weather, shorter lines in supermarkets, and increased tailwind for bicycle lanes, he garnered over 23,000 votes, enough for a seat in the national Parliament. He served his full four-year term.

TO COUNTER PERCEIVED RIGHT-WING, male chauvinism in Polish politics, a group of liberal women formed the Women's Party to fight the October 2007 general election. As part of their campaign to confront typical male attitudes to women, they chose the curious tactic of announcing their formation by having seven of their members pose naked behind a placard reading, "Everything for the future...and nothing to hide" that also covered their private parts. Not only did the poster cause outrage among the deeply conservative Catholic establishment, but also most observers concluded that it only reinforced Polish men's attitudes to the position of women. The party won just 0.28 percent of the vote and failed to secure a single seat.

MUSIKARI KOMBO, A KENYAN opposition MP, was unseated by the country's high court in November 1994 for having used witchcraft to win votes in his victory in the 1992 general election. Kombo, who won the Webuye constituency in the west of the country, had paid 70,000 shillings (about $830) to a local witch doctor to conduct a ceremony four days before the election, involving the killing of a ram and the aspiring candidate sitting in its intestines dressed only in underpants.

The ejection turned out to be only a temporary setback.

He was back in the seat in 1997 and eventually became a minister for another 10 years in Parliament.

 THE NARROW LOSER IN Romania's presidential election in December 2009 blamed the malignant effect of a government-sponsored mind controller as the cause of his defeat. Opposition candidate Mircea Geoana, who lost by just 70,000 votes in a 10 million voter turnout, called for the result to be nullified after television footage showed a shadowy character dogging him at various campaign visits. Identifying him as Aliodor Manolea, a well-known parapsychologist, journalists then turned up multiple examples of his presence at key Geoana rallies, lurking unobtrusively in the background and fixing the candidate with a menacing stare. They also noticed that Manolea was almost permanently in the entourage of the incumbent president, Traian Basescu, and was with him when he celebrated his narrow victory. Geoana's wife publicly claimed that her husband had been hexed by the mystic, who had launched "negative energy attacks" on him. The president's office issued official statements denying the parapsychologist had been part of the official campaign, but—a point seized on

by conspiracy theorists—was unable to explain why he had appeared so often in the strictly controlled crowds around the president.

SOMERSET MAN CHRIS BYRNE was elected to nine different councils in May 2007 without having a single vote cast for him. As the only candidate in each of the nine seats, he did not require any voter actually to cast a ballot in his favor. He was nominated for positions on Axbridge town council, parish councils for Cheddar, Rooksbridge, Compton Bishop, Weare, Banwell, and Draycott, as well as two more on Sedgmoor district council. He claimed he would not be overstretched in his duties, saying, "I am very organized."

AN INDIAN BUSINESSMEN, NAMED only as K. Padmarajan, secured the unenviable title of the world's least successful politician in April 2001 when he stood for a seat in the southern state of Tamil Nadu, having failed in 44 previous attempts at election. He lost. Recognized by the Indian edition of the *Guinness Book of World Records*, he has continued his efforts unrelentingly. When last heard of, in November 2009, he had just registered for a state by-election, his 103rd election contest. He is not thought to have won.

OLEH PERKOV, WHO FAILED in his bid to become mayor of the Ukrainian city of Zaporizhia in June 2003, castrated himself after receiving fewer than a hundred votes in the election. The head of a local research institute, Perkov told local press that he had cut off his testicles because of the "humiliating defeat." He was reported to be in stable condition after doctors operated to repair the damage.

SO CLOSE YET SO FAR

Herbert Connolly campaigned to the last moment in his 1988 effort to retain his seat on the Massachusetts Governor's Council. He lost track of time and arrived to cast his own vote 15 minutes after his polling station had closed. He polled 14,715 votes to his opponent's 14,716, and thus lost by his own single uncast vote.

DOMINIC VOLPE, CAMPAIGNING IN 2007 to be a legislator for Westchester County, Virginia, lost critical ground a few days before polling day when his team inadvertently dialed automated telephone calls to thousands of residents soliciting their vote—at 2 a.m. It may have cost him dear indeed. He lost the election by 4,394 votes to 4,302, a margin of just 92.

In June 2004, Noel Carino was formally declared the winner of a tightly contested 2001 general election seat in the Philippines' lower house, the House of Representatives. Legal challenges on questionable ballots had taken nearly three years to settle, including his opponent appealing all the way to the country's Supreme Court. The court finally pronounced Carino the winner two days before Parliament ended its session. He was sworn in the next day, to serve a solitary day as elected representative before the House was dissolved for the next elections. "Better late than never," the House speaker was reported to have told him.

SCARY CONTESTS

One of the most entertaining elections of recent years was the battle in 2000 for the Berkeley County seat in the South Carolina House of Representatives. It pitted sitting member Mrs. Shirley Hinson against her husband of 32 years, James. The couple was gripped in a bitter divorce battle, and the campaign descended into little more than a public marital fight. Mr. Hinson used the campaign to pour out his divorce case. He accused his wife of having an affair with another state politician. He had earlier been charged by police with making death threats to the person cited.

Mrs. H. vehemently denied any romantic involvement. The couple's divorce papers were widely, and anonymously, faxed to the local press and radio stations. Campaign broadcasts ostensibly to the electorate turned into personal vendettas. Mrs. Hinson accused her opponent of being "a self-serving, mean, vindictive individual who will do anything to get a result." He retaliated by warning the voters, "You have to be very careful of a pretty face."

Mrs. Hinson won the contest with a 42 percent vote to his 32 percent. Four years later she married the politician with whom she had denied having the affair.

WILLIAM LEVINGER, RUNNING AS the Republican nominee for election to the U.S. House of Representatives in Idaho in 1996, spent most of the final six weeks of his campaign holed up in a state mental institution after spectacularly imploding during a television interview. For reasons only he himself could know, halfway through the interview he propositioned the female reporter, offering her $5,000 if she would kiss him on camera. He then began stripping off his clothes. The station cut the broadcast when he was down to his underpants. Despite the restrictive circumstances of his last weeks of electioneering, he still managed to win 32 percent of the vote on polling day.

IN APRIL 2010, ANDREW Romanoff, the Democratic candidate campaigning for a Senate seat in Colorado, admitted having doctored a photograph of one of his rallies posted on his website by adding black and Latino supporters to the crowd to appear prominently alongside him. Romanoff, who is white, claimed that the image was modified "to improve the illustration," calling any other interpretation—like deceiving voters about the level of support he had from minorities—"outrageous and reprehensible." He initially stuck to this defense. Within 48 hours he had pulled the picture.

ED MATTS, THE CONSERVATIVE candidate for Dorset South in the 2005 general election, was found to have doctored an old photograph of himself with leading Tory Ann Widdecombe, and reversed the messages to make him look tough on immigrants and appeal to the current anti-immigration sentiment of his party's campaign. The original shot showed Matts and Widdecombe campaigning on behalf of a Malawian asylum-seeking family. Looking concerned and not a little pious, the pair carried placards with a photograph of the woman and her four children along with a plea to "let them stay." The new photograph showed the pair still as concerned, but with placards reading "Controlled

Immigration" and "Not Chaos and Inhumanity." Matts apologized for the deception. He failed to win the seat.

JACOB REES-MOGG, THE CONSERVATIVE prospective candidate for North East Somerset, was revealed to have run a publicity campaign calling for "more honesty" in politics in 2009 by using a leaflet with a faked photograph. The handout, which purported to show him talking with "a woman in the village of Midsomer Norton," turned out to show him with a member of staff from his own finance company posing as the concerned citizen. The leaflet piously told readers how "Jacob Rees-Mogg believes it is time to be honest with North Somerset residents." Despite the exposé, Rees-Mogg increased his party's majority when he won the constituency in the 2010 general election.

IN JULY 2003, NORWAY repealed its law that had banned intoxicated persons from voting in elections.

ALL FOR NOTHING

After months of energetic campaigning in the 2000 election to the city council of Southwest Ranches, a suburb of Fort Lauderdale, Florida, a candidate spent his last week begging the electorate not to vote for him. Doug Couvertier, a fire chief in nearby Miami-Dade County, signed up for the election unaware that the rules of Miami-Dade forbade county employees from running for public office unless they took leave of absence and resigned if they won. "If I win, I'll be fired from my job," he told reporters. "In three more years, I can retire." When he realized his dilemma, and was also told that it was too late to take his name off the ballot, the election took on a bizarre hue as friends rallied round to dissuade electors from voting for him. Vince Falletta, running for mayor, promised, "I'll make every effort to see that he's not elected, so his job and pension won't be jeopardized." In the end, Couvertier lost by a landslide. He got just 74 votes of the 1,700 cast.

ORGANIZERS OF THE 2010 election for county court judge in Galveston, Texas, created a bureaucratic nightmare for candidates when they mistakenly set the deadline for nominations to come after the state's legal deadline for withdrawing them. When Trey Dibrell, a judge for 16 years, changed his mind about wanting to stand again and decided to retract his name from the ballot in early January, he was told that the deadline for being able to do so had already passed, even though there were still six days to go before the closing date for nominations. He began a "don't vote for me" campaign before taking his case to the courts. A judge granted him his wish to have his name deleted.

JOE SELLE, RUNNING UNOPPOSED in April 2007 for reelection to his seat on the city council of Missouri City, Missouri (a small hamlet of 300), failed to get any votes at all. He did not even vote for himself as he had forgotten when election day was. So, apparently, had all the other 34 people registered to vote in his district. The potential awkwardness of a "no result" was solved by the city's legal advisor confirming that under the city's charter, incumbents kept their seats unless another person was elected in their place. The thrill of small-town politics was clearly stronger in Selle's neighboring district: the turnout there was two.

SIMILAR PROBLEMS AFFECTED THE race for mayor and council in the North Dakota community of Pillsbury (population 24) in 2008 when the whole town either forgot or was too busy to vote. It could have been because current mayor Darrel Brudevold was standing unopposed, and his wife and another councilor also had no opponents for their two alderman seats, but not one single elector managed to cast their ballot. "We usually get half a dozen making it to the polls," said Brudevold. He had planned to vote but he had crops to tend. His wife, who doubled as postmistress and local beauty salon owner, was also too busy to get to the polling station. Under the rules, incumbents could stay in their positions until the next election.

STATE LAW IN MISSISSIPPI was different back in 1991. Denny James was the only candidate in one ward in elections for the town council of Centerville. At counting time it emerged that not a single person had voted, not even the candidate himself. As the law required a candidate to obtain at least one vote before being elected, a rerun had to be called. He got 45 the next time.

ANIMATED CONTESTS

The 400 residents of the Californian town of Sunol elected Bosco, an eight-year-old Rottweiler-Labrador mix, as their mayor in 1981. He beat two human candidates for the post. He remained mayor unbeaten for 13 years until he died. In 2008, a bronze statue of the dog was unveiled and dedicated in the main street. It was a rather more fitting memorial than the one that had been installed when a new restaurant named Bosco's Bones and Brew opened in 1999. Its owner chose to memorialize the former mayor with a specially engineered life-size model of the dog planted on the bar. To draw a pint, the bartender lifted the dog's left rear leg and the beer came out from...you can guess where.

THE REMOTE WESTERN TEXAS border town of Lajitas (population 100) elected a goat as its mayor in 1986. Clay Henry started off a veritable dynasty as, when he died in 1992, one of his offspring succeeded him in the post, to be followed by Clay Henry III. All became icons locally for their beer-drinking exploits, mainly exhibited for tourists. Clay Henry Sr. lived to be 23, and then spent years on display at the local store, stuffed and with a beer bottle in his mouth. By the time it came to the third incumbent, rivalry had developed. Clay Henry III only won in 2000 after a battle against a dog called Buster and a wooden Indian statue.

UNUSUAL OUTCOMES

Angela Tuttle found herself elected constable in Hancock County, Tennessee, in 2008 merely because she turned up to vote. There were no candidates on the ballot, and thus her write-in vote for herself carried the election.

ROSAMUND ROCYN-JONES, A CANDIDATE for a seat on the Grosmont village council in local elections in Wales in 1983, found herself elected even though she lost the contest. After a night of four recounts and "two double-checks" showed she and her opponent were tied, the returning officer got them to draw lots. Rocyn-Jones's opponent, Trevor Sayce-Davies, picked the winning slip of paper, but the returning officer, who later blamed lack of sleep, then announced the wrong victor. No one else at the count apparently noticed the mistake. Lawyers advised that technically the losing Mrs. Rocyn-Jones was the lawful councilor. It took a court case in front of two senior judges two months later to correct the mistake.

AN OBSCURE NEW PARTY managed to win a seat in Paraguay's national elections in May 1998 by calling itself the "Partido Blanco" (White Party). It achieved most of its 35,000 votes because of alleged confusion among those in the electorate who intended to cast "blank" votes, a peculiar provision of Paraguayan procedure allowing electors to register a "none-of-the above" choice. Analysts feared that many had stamped the White Party's box instead of the "blank vote" option. The ruse appeared to have capitalized on a country where 60 percent of the population were classified as functionally illiterate.

Singapore was able to announce the outcome of its general election in October 2001 nine days before polling day—without any hint of malpractice. So few of the opposition bothered to challenge the ruling People's Action Party, which had been in power in the city-state since independence in 1965, that fewer than half the seats faced contested elections when nominations closed just over a week before polling was due. With 55 members already returned unopposed out of the 84-strong assembly, Prime Minister Goh Chok Tong sailed into a further six years of office before even the first ballot was cast.

Israeli election law preventing political candidates being shown on television within a month of polling day led to bizarre coverage of Prime Minister Menachem Begin's vital summit meeting with Egyptian president Sadat in June 1981. While viewers could see all of Sadat, the only evidence of Begin's presence was a dismembered hand, or Sadat talking studiously to a shoulder or an elbow. Broadcasting chiefs branded the rule "ludicrous." Perversely, viewers could switch channels to neighboring Jordanian television and see unrestricted coverage.

In 1996, Japan's electoral laws forbidding the alteration of approved election material meant that TV advertisements for former health minister Saburo Toida, who had died during the campaign, had to continue to appear until the end of the election, even though his son had succeeded him as candidate.

THAILAND SET THE EXTREME record for electoral neutrality in March 2000 when it held the first elections for the country's Senate (members had previously been appointed by the government). To combat the country's notorious record for vote buying and corruption, the electoral commission banned all forms of campaigning, all political broadcasts, and all political debates. The law, which only allowed candidates to introduce themselves to the public, forbade them from expressing any political affiliation or viewpoint, or from using a microphone in public.

It still produced chaos. Amid accusations of widespread cheating, more than a third of the results were nullified by the commission in the days after the election. Only 122 were declared to have been settled cleanly. Reruns had to be held the following month, and for 12 seats, a second rerun was ordered. Finally, on July 27, the commission was able to announce the confirmation of the 200th, and final, senator.

The experiment was widely seen as a farce and was destined not to be repeated. By 2007, a military coup had thrown out the old order and reestablished more traditional arrangements. The Senate was now smaller (175) and only half of the seats were to be elected.

CLOSE CALLS

The 1998 election for the mayor of the small New Mexico town of Estancia was settled in local fashion when incumbent James Farrington and his challenger JoAnn Carlson tied on 68 votes each. Under the state's rules, the election was decided by a game of chance—a five-card draw from a pack of cards. Farrington won with ace high.

ONE OF THE CLOSEST elections on record was the 1994 contest for a seat on the city council in Rice, Minnesota. Virgil Nelson and Mitch Fiedler tied at 90 votes each, so went into the tiebreaker of drawing cards. The first attempt produced a pair of eights. Astonishingly, in the redraw, both produced aces. At the third attempt, Nelson drew a seven, to be outdone by Fiedler who drew…an eight. Fiedler later went on to become mayor and, at the time of writing, is still at the helm.

CONSERVATIVE CANDIDATE RICHARD BLUNT was awarded his seat on the Leicestershire County Council three months and a court case after the election in November 1991 had ended in a tie. The returning officer had initially resolved the impasse by drawing lots, and Blunt's Labor Party opponent, Derek Wintle, won out. A single ballot was at issue. It had been rejected as invalid because the voter had marked the choice not with a cross but with a tick, a smiley face, and the words "yes, please." Under electoral law, any ballot was disqualified if written on, as it might lead to the possible identification of the voter. A court hearing the following February, dismissing the fears on this occasion, ruled the ballot to be legal, one official commenting, "It's obvious it's no Gainsborough. It bears a passing resemblance to Dennis the Menace."

ADHERENCE TO THE RULES reached extreme lengths in 2006 when the tied election for a seat on the school board in Adak, Alaska, was settled by the toss of a coin—even though one of the two candidates was dead. Katherine Dunton won, even though she had died on polling day. State law did not allow her rival to win by default.

 GETTING THE VOTE OUT
To address voting apathy among its community, representatives on the municipal council in Lierne,

near Trondheim in Norway, decided in August 1995 to make everyone who voted in the following month's local election eligible for an all-expenses-paid holiday to a Mediterranean resort.

VOTERS IN SIBERIA WERE encouraged to cast their ballots in elections to the Yakutia regional council in the depths of winter in January 2002 by having all votes entered into a lottery with the chance to win a car or a television set. Turnout was boosted to an unusually high 70 percent.

TO TRY TO REPAIR Arizona's notoriously low voter turnout—usually just above 50 percent, one of the lowest in America—voters considered a proposal in 2006 for giving a $1 million prize to a random elector in each two-yearly election as an incentive to increase participation. The brainchild of Mark Osterloh, a past runner (unsuccessfully) for state governor, the idea obtained 185,000 signatures, well past the required level to get on the ballot in the November elections, where it was, perhaps surprisingly, defeated by a two-to-one majority by Arizonans. Critics worried that it would encourage people to think even less about who they voted for.

CAMPAIGNING IN THE 1979 British general election, Swindon Conservative candidate Nigel Hammond discovered the long memories of voters. A 94-year-old woman in a retirement home told him she would not be voting for his party because after the First World War they had campaigned to hang the German kaiser but had not kept their promise.

GEOFFREY FINSBERG, THE CONSERVATIVE candidate in Hampstead and Highgate in the 1983 general election, is believed to have set a record when he addressed a campaign meeting attended by just one member of the public.

THE FIRST DIRECT ELECTIONS to the European Parliament in June 1979 struggled to attract public interest, achieving an average turnout across the UK of a mere 33 percent. The Birmingham *Evening Mail* reported the extremely slow start at one polling station in the Birmingham South constituency where by lunchtime only one ballot had been cast. An 83-year-old woman was responsible, but there were doubts whether she really knew what she was doing. An official reported that she had declared that her vote was unlikely to help England win as "Israel has already won." It transpired she thought she was voting for the Eurovision Song Contest—an annual song contest among countries in the European Union—and had arrived at the polling station clutching a copy of the *Radio Times* open at the voting page. The song contest had been held three months earlier.

ORGANIZATIONAL HICCUPS

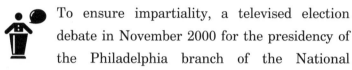 To ensure impartiality, a televised election debate in November 2000 for the presidency of the Philadelphia branch of the National Association for the Advancement of Colored People installed a cardboard cut-out of one of three candidates after he had phoned in saying he could not make the broadcast because of a family emergency. The channel, WTVE-TV, propped up a life-size figure of Thomas Logan in a chair to comply with national election rules on equal representation.

BROWARD COUNTY IN FLORIDA, the center of the storm in the disputed 2000 U.S. presidential election, encountered fresh mishaps in congressional elections in 2002. Despite spending $2.5 million over the summer to correct faulty electronic voting machines that had delayed primary election results in March by a week, in the November election over 103,000 ballots—nearly a quarter of the entire vote—were misplaced and not counted. They were discovered almost a week after polling day. Officials claimed the extra ballots did not change the outcome of the election, which had already been declared.

ELECTIONS IN THE KURDISH region of northern Iraq in 1992 had to be postponed when German-gifted supplies of indelible ink designed to prevent voter fraud were found to be easily soluble in water. The ink was a donation from the German state of North Rhine-Westphalia, and part of the West's post-Gulf War effort to restore political life in the breakaway area. The problem was only noticed when a trial run, held the day before voting was due, revealed that instead of setting hard in minutes the ink was removable "with a bit of spit and scrubbing." "We all trusted German efficiency," said Hoshyar Zebari, an election official.

INDIA'S ELECTIONS COMMISSIONER, G.V.G. Krishnamurthy, tasked with overseeing arrangements for the country's 1999 election, found himself barred from voting when he arrived at his own polling station, as his name was missing from the electoral register that his office was responsible for compiling.

A CHILEAN MAN WHOM election officials had repeatedly denied the right to vote on the grounds that records showed he was dead, announced to the press in December 1999 that he was tired of arguing his case and declared he would never try to vote again. At 61 years old, Ernesto Alvear had just been prevented from voting in the country's presidential election in his home city of Valparaiso. It was the third election from which he had been barred. Officially, the state regarded him as having been dead for the past 10 years. The mix-up had originally been caused by the death of a man with an identical name, causing Alvear to spend a decade in a bureaucratic nightmare trying to prove to the authorities he was alive.

TO ENSURE NO ONE was impeded from participating in its second all-race general election in 1999, South African election authorities built a special polling station for Lincolnshire Farm in the remote Drakensburg Mountains region of the Free State province to cater to the single registered voter in the area. The elector did not show up to vote.

IN A 1990 STATE by-election in Queensland, Australia, the opposition Labor Party withdrew a planned advertising campaign that would ridicule the outgoing member's claims of innocence on corruption charges by a series of posters showing Don Lane with a progressively longer Pinocchio-type nose. It scrapped the campaign when it learned that Lane had entered the hospital—for a nasal complaint.

ORGANIZATIONAL HEADACHES

Gerrymandering—the artificial drawing of constituency boundaries to gain electoral advantage—reached such extreme proportions in some parts of the United States that the Supreme Court eventually ruled in 1997 that a constituency in New York was so bizarrely drawn as to be unconstitutional. The 12th Congressional District in New York, which stretched from Brooklyn to Queens to the Lower East Side of Manhattan, was drawn specifically to collect sufficient ethnic Hispanic voters together to guarantee a victory for a Hispanic candidate. According to court testimony, the borders of the sinuous three-pronged district changed direction 813 times. The Supreme Court ruled that it breached the Constitution's guarantee of equal treatment.

It was not the only extreme example of the practice. In the 2002 midterm elections, political analysts estimated that the boundaries had been so manipulated in America's House of Representatives districts that of the 435 seats only between 16 and 35—less than 8 percent—produced genuine competition between opposing parties. In the end, only four incumbents lost to challengers, producing a 99 percent return rate for sitting members. Around 80 percent of seats were won by a margin of more than 20 percentage points and some 200 seats, nearly half, were won by more than 40. Eighty seats were uncontested, producing a state of affairs where only around 10 percent of American electors live in seats where their vote actually stands a chance of making a difference. By the 2004 elections, experts estimated that only 29 of the 435 seats were genuinely contestable between the parties, with 68 seats being uncontested.

In contrast to the salamander that spawned the original phrase for the practice adopted by Governor Gerry of Massachusetts in the early nineteenth century, drawers of modern constituencies could use computer-aided analysis and mapping to select areas of similar political hue. As a result, in the words of one report, districts resemble "scorpions or amoeba—sprouting long tails and tentacles," to take in neighborhoods of one's preferred political complexion. Two districts in Chicago—the 11th and 17th—both appeared to be several large blocks spread either the length or breadth of town, tenuously connected by thin corridors. Their narrow ends did indeed resemble scorpion pincers squaring up to each other.

One of the most notorious examples was North Carolina's 12th district, created in 1992 when the state was awarded an extra seat due to population increases. It was designed as a black majority seat and snakes for nearly 100 miles across the state northeastward from the city of Charlotte up to Winston-Salem, taking in portions of five other cities on the way. At some points it is no wider than a highway lane. On its creation, the *Wall Street Journal* labeled the district "political pornography." At the time of going to press, it had been represented in Congress by the same individual since its inaugural election in 1993.

Another extreme example is California's 23rd district, which hugs the coastline in the southern part of the state for over 200 miles from San Luis Obispo County and rarely intrudes more than five miles inland. All parts of the seat are only completely connected when the tide goes out.

IN ELECTIONS FOR THE Indian state of Kamataka in February 1985, 301 candidates ran for one seat. The ballot, printed on both sides, was the size of a table top.

ELECTIONS FOR THE 55 seats on the city council in Prague in November 1994 were run as a single constituency vote. It required a ballot 40 inches by 28 inches to list all 1,187 candidates. The ballot had to be sent to each registered voter—all 1,018,527 of them.

A BALLOT 42 INCHES wide and 30 inches long, nick-named "the "tablecloth ballot," was required for the election to the New South Wales Senate in March 1999, when 264 people ran, representing 81 parties or groups, for the 21 seats available. The state electoral commission was forced to double the size of its voting booths, build bigger ballot boxes, and contract a special printer to produce the forms. Tagged "the ballot paper from Hell," some politicians feared that it had the effect of deterring people from actually making their own choices, opting for voting "above the line," which allowed the parties to distribute preferences as they chose. After the election, New South Wales changed its electoral laws to make it more difficult for so many aspirants to stand in future.

THE INTRODUCTION OF PROPORTIONAL representation, and a concern for fairness, produced a ballot in Italy's 2006 election that was over five feet wide. The 48 parties contending were all listed horizontally instead of vertically after evidence that those at the top of lists running down the page tended to be favored by most voters, who could not be bothered to get to the end.

TAKING DEFEAT GRACEFULLY

The bitter 2000 U.S. presidential election between George W. Bush and Al Gore, which eventually had to be settled by a Supreme Court ruling after five weeks of dispute over confusing ballots in Florida, left more physical marks as the Democratic regime vacated the White House. Republican staff arriving to take over offices in January 2001 found that their predecessors had removed the W keys from "dozens, if not hundreds" of computer keyboards according to Ari Fleischer, the new White House spokesperson, preventing the new president's name from being typed fully. Other acts of vandalism were reported, including obscene messages left in photocopiers and on answering machines, telephone cables cut, and filing cabinets glued shut. Another trick was for departees to reroute their phones automatically and randomly to other government offices. Fleischer graciously rose above the fray, commenting, "The president understands that transitions can be times of difficulty and strong emotions. And he's going to approach it in that vein."

FROM THE HISTORY BOOKS

In the annals of bizarre elections, few will ever match the notorious 1927 presidential election in Liberia, which has gone down in the *Guinness Book of World Records* as the most fraudulent in history. Charles Dunbar Burgess King retained his presidency by defeating Thomas Faulkner with an official majority of 234,000. The only trouble was that there were only 15,000 registered electors at the time.

SIR HENRY GRAYSON, ELECTED in 1918 for the Conservatives in Birkenhead, and reported to have been considered the best-looking member of the House of Commons, is reputed to be the only MP returned in modern times without having made a single election speech in his campaign. He still won a 10,000 majority.

ROBERT TURTON WAS ELECTED Conservative MP for Thirsk and Malton in 1929 during the Great Depression after taking over the campaign following the sudden death of his uncle, the sitting member, who died on nomination day. He went on to hold the seat until retirement in 1974 and his elevation to the House of Lords as Lord Tranmire. His rapid selection was fortuitous. It was said the party was worried about the extra costs of changing its candidate. Choosing the nephew saved them the cost of reprinting the "Vote Turton" posters.

PETERBOROUGH MP HARMAR NICHOLLS holds the record for enduring probably the least secure parliamentary career. Although he won the seat in 1950 and successfully defended it at seven general elections, he needed a total of 21 recounts along the way. His initial victory was by the slender majority of just 144 votes. In 1966, it took seven recounts before he was declared winner—by a mere three votes. In February 1974, he needed 4 recounts to establish he had scraped through again, by 22. He finally lost out in the October election of that year, going down by a hefty 1,848.

ON TWO OCCASIONS AROUND the world, national elections have been won by the closest possible margin. In the January 1961 general election on Zanzibar, the Afro-Shirazi Party secured a majority of one seat, having won the seat of Chake-Chake by a single vote. After elections in the Cook Islands in the Pacific in June 1999, the coalition government of the Cook Islands Party and the New Alliance Party enjoyed a 13–12 majority in the legislature. Its lead rested on the contested result in the seat of Pukapuka, which had been won by one vote. An election court ruled the result invalid in September, depriving the government of its short-lived majority.

WHILE CAMPAIGNING FOR U.S. president in 1912, Theodore Roosevelt was shot in an attempted assassination as he left his hotel in Milwaukee for a rally. Despite being wounded in the chest, he refused to abandon his planned speech. He appeared on stage with blood oozing from his shirt. Starting by saying he hoped his audience would excuse him for making a shorter speech than intended, he spoke for an hour and a half before being taken off to the hospital. He still lost the election, and carried the bullet in him for the rest of his life.

ODDEST OF ALL CANDIDATES perhaps was Thaddeus Stevens, U.S. congressman from Philadelphia, who died in 1868 and whose corpse was nominated by the Republican Party for reelection to the House of Representatives as a tribute to his Civil War service. He was elected eight weeks after being buried.

RADIO BROADCASTING IN ELECTIONS began in earnest after the Second World War. In marked contrast to our modern sound-bite times, Prime Minister Winston Churchill was firm with the BBC in the 1945 election when it had asked him to keep his first election broadcast to only(!) 20 minutes: "I insisted on at least half an hour."

FRANKLIN ROOSEVELT, CAMPAIGNING FOR reelection as president in 1936, engaged in a radio debate with Alf Landon, his Republican challenger. Each had ten minutes to make a speech. Roosevelt went first, spoke for three minutes and then fell silent for the rest of his allotted time. By the time it was Landon's turn to talk, most of the audience had switched off.

LIECHTENSTEIN ALLOWED WOMEN TO vote in elections only as recently as 1984, the last country in Europe to grant suffrage to women. Switzerland granted it only in 1971 and Andorra in 1970. Four Middle East states have recently relented after centuries of exclusion—Qatar (1997), Oman (2003), Kuwait (2005), and the United Arab Emirates (2006). There remains no right of women's suffrage in Saudi Arabia and Vatican City.

3

THE (MIS)RULE OF LAW: LEGISLATORS

Electors rightly expect their legislators to be giving their full attention to the most important affairs of state. But even in the course of "normal" business, the workings of a government can involve many strange practices.

HONORABLE MEMBERS

Until its repeal in 2000, section 10(j) of the 1963 Electoral Act of Western Samoa contained the rule that any member of Parliament who had sex with a person other than their spouse was to be disqualified from holding their seat. As recently as 1982 a member was expelled on these grounds.

PRESIDENT MARCOS ORDERED THE title of members of the Philippine National Assembly be changed in 1984 from

Assemblyman to Mambabatas Pambansa (MP) so that the abbreviation appearing on name plates was no longer "Ass."

THE CLARITY OF LAW

Irish legislators passed the 1984 Road Traffic (Insurance) Disc Regulations, Section 4 of which stated, "Every insurance disc shall be in the shape of a rectangle."

AN UNNOTICED MISTAKE IN an Arkansas law on marriage age introduced in 2007 temporarily enabled anyone in the state—even babies—to marry. What was designed to set a minimum age for marriage without parental consent was given the opposite effect by the typo, which was only discovered after the provision had been signed into law. A key section, intended to require girls who were under the age of 18 and pregnant to have to show parental consent for the marriage, was found to have a rogue "not" in the clause, which effectively enabled anyone to marry with their parents' blessing. It read: "In order for a person who is younger than eighteen (18) years of age and who is not pregnant to obtain a marriage license, the person must provide the county clerk with evidence of parental consent to the marriage." The Arkansas legislature had to repeal the law in April 2008 and start all over again.

SOUTH AUSTRALIA DISCOVERED IN 2002 that the state was still officially at war when embarrassed parliamentary authorities found that successive state governments had forgotten to repeal the Emergency Powers Act introduced in 1941 to manage business during the Second World War. No one had issued the formal proclamation required under the law to end the war, and the act remained in force. On August 16, Premier Mike Rann proclaimed the end of the conflict, explaining that the legal quirk was due to the fact that the act was to have expired automatically with the expected peace treaties at the end of the war but, with the onset of the Cold War, no such peace treaty was ever achieved. "It seems we are the only state in Australia with wartime legislation like this still on the books." The act was formally, and hastily, repealed with immediate effect.

THE IRISH PARLIAMENT WAS required to pass a special law in December 1988 to resolve the problem of a judge who had forgotten his date of birth. Three years earlier, District Justice Seamus Mahon, who presided at Portlaoise in County Laois, had duly applied for dispensation from the retirement age of 65 believing that the age deadline had just fallen for him. In fact, he had been born a year earlier than he thought, meaning his exemption was a year too late and technically invalid, as were the 120,000-odd judgments he had continued to make in the years that followed. The special act gave retrospective authority to all his decisions.

During the passage of the 1990 Broadcasting Act, the House of Lords found itself having to pronounce on the tricky issue of a legal definition of "pop music." It was necessary because the proposed legislation aimed to ensure that only one of the three franchises being set up by the act would be for pop, so their lordships tackled the (to them) obscure subject in one of the more surreal debates ever held in the Lords.

Earl Ferrers, minister of state at the Home Office in charge of steering the measure through, confessed that he had lost his own attempt to describe the matter at hand as "thump, thump, thump." This had been judged by legal draftsmen to "not be statutorily or parliamentarily adequate." Instead, he proposed—and peers agreed—that the formal 61-word legal definition would be: "Pop music includes rock music and other kinds of modern popular music which are characterized by a strong rhythmic element and a reliance on electronic amplification for their performance, whether or not, in the case of any particular piece of rock or other such music, the music in question enjoys a current popularity as measured by the number of recordings sold."

STRANGE LAWMAKING

New Mexico state senator Duncan Scott waged a campaign in 1995 in protest of the growing trend of defendants pleading insanity in courts to avoid criminal convictions. Evidently no admirer of the psychiatric profession that helped them do this, he proposed amending state law to require that:

When a psychologist or psychiatrist testifies during a defendant's competency hearing, the psychologist or psychiatrist shall wear a cone-shaped hat that is not less than two feet tall. The surface of the hat shall be imprinted with stars and lightning bolts.

Additionally, the psychologist or psychiatrist shall be required to don a white beard that is not less than eighteen inches in length, and shall punctuate crucial elements in his testimony by stabbing the air with a wand.

Whenever a psychologist or psychiatrist provides expert testimony regarding the defendant's testimony, the bailiff shall dim the courtroom lights and administer two strikes to a Chinese gong.

In March of that year the amendment was approved by the Senate without a vote, and passed by the House of Representatives 46–14. It took a veto by Governor Gary Johnson to stop it becoming law.

THE U.S. STATE OF Louisiana made lack of respect of teachers from schoolchildren formally illegal in a controversial 1999 law that came into force at the start of the new school year in September. The measure made it a legal requirement for all children in school from the ages of 5 to 10 to call their teachers "sir" or "ma'am." The state, already notorious for the severity of its laws on abortion and divorce, was the first in the country to adopt legislation in the area. Both houses of the state legislature passed the law with overwhelming support, despite teachers' objections that it ridiculed their authority.

THE FRENCH NATIONAL ASSEMBLY adopted similar legislation in the summer of 2002, making it possible for schoolchildren to be sent to prison for up to six months for insulting their teachers. Prosecutions could be started against children who "attack the dignity or respect due" to their teachers. In addition to prison, a fine up to €7,500 (about $9,650) could be imposed. The law notionally applied to children as young as 13, although officials said it would almost certainly be limited in practice to older students. Teachers expressed concern at the apparently draconian nature of the law and described the move as "window dressing."

IN MARCH 2003, THE New Mexico legislature approved Representative Dan Foley's proposal for a law to designate an official "Extraterrestrial Culture Day," to be celebrated on the second Thursday of each February. Foley, from the New Mexico town of Roswell, renowned in UFO folklore for a supposed alien landing in 1947, introduced the legislation to recognize, in the words of the statute, the "many visitations, sightings, unexplained mysteries, attributed technological advances, experimentations, expeditions, explorations, intrigues, provision of story lines for Hollywood epics, and other accomplishments of alien beings throughout the universe that have contributed to New Mexico's worldwide recognition as a unique and dynamic mosaic of cultural anomalies." The day would be observed "to celebrate and honor all past, present and future extraterrestrial visitors in ways to enhance relationships among all the citizens of the cosmos, known and unknown."

IN APRIL 2003, THE Oregon House of Representatives passed a law the sole purpose of which was to define "science" ("the systematic enterprise of gathering knowledge about the universe and organizing and condensing that knowledge into testable laws and theories"). The sponsor of the measure, Betsy Close, was understood to believe that establishing the particular formulation in state law would constrain local environmental activists, who had become successful in lodging "scientific" evidence to challenge government activities.

THE GEORGIA HOUSE OF Representatives passed a measure in 2004 requiring all buildings owned by the state, counties, or cities to have twice as many women's toilets as men's to even up one of life's perennial practical inequalities. The state Senate failed to concur and the legislation died.

GUN-TOTING TEXAS PASSED LEGISLATION, which was signed into law by Governor Rick Perry in June 2007, allowing blind people to hunt with guns. The proposal had passed both houses of the legislature unanimously. The only requirement to ensure wider public safety was that the sightless hunter had to be accompanied by someone who was not legally blind, who owned a hunting license, and who was at least 13 years old.

TEXAS STATE REPRESENTATIVE JAMES Kaster from the border town of El Paso introduced a proposed law into the state assembly's 1974 session that would require all criminals to give their victims 24 hours' notice of their intended crime. The notice could be given orally (such as by telephone call) or in writing. It would also require the criminal to acknowledge their acceptance of the victims' right to exercise lethal force in their defense. The measure failed to win approval.

 IN MARCH 1978, OKLAHOMA state representative Cleta Deatherage introduced an amendment in protest of an antiabortion bill in her state assembly. It would require men to seek written consent from a woman before having sex, and that before granting permission the woman should receive a warning about the risks of pregnancy and the dangers of childbirth. Should the woman be illiterate, the warning would need to be read to her (in her native language). The proposal was unsurprisingly defeated, but the result, 78–9, meant that nearly 12 percent of the members taking part supported the idea.

GERMAN LEGISLATORS HAVE CONSIDERED three times since 2003 proposals to give the vote to babies. A move in

September 2003 to entitle parents to cast an extra vote on behalf of each child until they were 18 failed to win support in the Bundestag, the national Parliament. The measure would have legally obliged parents to explain political affairs to their offspring and to comply with their voting wishes. With under-18s accounting for 20 percent of the population, sponsors extolled the virtues of widening the franchise.

IN 1976, STATE LEGISLATOR Michael Connolly formally introduced into the Massachusetts House of Representatives a proposed law that would sell the state back to Native Americans. The draft bill required Massachusetts to be auctioned off on January 3, 1977. His fellow lawmakers failed to back the measure.

PARLIAMENTARY DECORUM

Karlene Maywald, a South Australian MP, was reprimanded by the state assembly speaker in October 2003 for using the word "please," ruling that it represented begging and claiming that it had been banned in parliamentary practice for 300 years. When she asked at question time whether the minister "could please advise the House" on water restrictions, Speaker Peter Lewis ruled her language out of order.

"The word 'please' is to beg, no honorable member in this place needs to beg any minister for anything, least of all an answer," he told MPs. Maywald expressed astonishment at being upbraided: "I was only being polite."

A month later, Speaker Lewis invited more controversy by ruling that energy minister Pat Conlon's use of "bloody" during a heated exchange was in order. "'Bloody' is an oath, 'by our lady,' arising from the ancient English of Chaucer," he opined, and thus ruled it entirely acceptable.

THE CITY COUNCIL OF Palo Alto, California, spent an evening in May 2003 debating a proposal from one of its committees that, if passed, would have banned "body language or other nonverbal methods of expression, disagreement or disgust" during council meetings. Aimed at enhancing decorum in debates, the measure, which had taken a year to develop and had already been inconclusively considered in a five-hour session two months earlier, sought to stop councilors using disparaging gestures. These, according to the new rules, would have included frowning, rolling the eyes, shaking the head, and sticking out the tongue.

The idea attracted such ridicule from the local community that as it turns out, even the head of the committee that proposed the rules voted against the idea, and they were thrown out unanimously.

BEYOND UNDERSTANDING

The Missouri House of Representatives passed a 1,012-page law in 1995...designed to reduce paperwork in the state government.

AN EARLY DAY MOTION in the British House of Commons in January 2008 calling for the disestablishment of the Church of England appeared on the order paper numbered 666—the "Number of the Beast." The numbering of the motion was automatically generated and corresponded to the order in which it was tabled. The author, Liberal Democrat member Bob Russell, said, "It's incredible [it] should have acquired this significant number."

MARYLAND LEGISLATORS DECIDED IN 1962 to make jousting its official state sport. It remains so to this day.

THE OREGON SENATE VOTED in 1989 to make the hazelnut the official state nut, the first state in America to have one.

IN NEBRASKA, WHERE SINCE 1996 state law has allowed the

governor to declare official state items without the legis-lature first considering them, Ben Nelson signed a procla-mation in May 1998 declaring the state now had an official soft drink—Kool-Aid, a nationally celebrated powdered soft drink, invented in the state in 1927. Alongside the traditional state symbols of official bird, tree, and flower, Nebraska enjoys an official state rock (the prairie agate), official state fossil (the mammoth), official state grass (the little bluestem), and official state insect (the honeybee).

WHILE WEST VIRGINIA ENDURED an unenviable reputation as one of the poorest states of the union, with falling jobs numbers, high social deprivation, and low health and education standards, legislators in the state Senate spent much time and energy in February 2000 debating the merits of the dulcimer as the preferred candidate for selec-tion as their official state musical instrument. Senators passed a resolution in favor, causing intense controversy in the lower House of Representatives, which favored the fiddle. Such is the level of dispute that, as of 2010, the issue remains unresolved.

A SIMILAR TIME-CONSUMING DISPUTE broke out in 2002 when the historic Californian town of Bodie, a former

gold-mining settlement, won the support of state assemblyman Tim Leslie for designating the place California's
official state ghost town. The proposal was overwhelmingly supported in the lower house in May, but when it
advanced to the Senate it encountered opposition from a
rival historic park, Calico, a former silver-mining town,
also now a deserted ghost town and reliant on tourism
for survival. Fearful that granting the official designation
to Bodie would disadvantage it, Calico secured the support of its local senator Jim Brulte, who was unrepentant
about the basis for his loyalties. "I've been to Calico, and
I haven't been to the other place, so I'm going with what I
know." Months of wrangling followed. Compromises were
proposed. Calico would withdraw its opposition if Bodie
was merely designated "an" official state ghost town
rather than "the" official state ghost town. As this broke
all the traditions of settling on a single recipient, legislators applied themselves further. The "Great Ghost Town
Compromise of 2002" resulted. Bodie would be declared
the official "gold rush ghost town" of California, and Calico
would be enthroned later as the state's official "silver rush
ghost town." On September 4, the governor of California
signed the legislation adopting Bodie's new status. In
2005, legislation was passed that made Calico the official

state silver rush ghost town of California, and it was signed into effect by Governor Arnold Schwarzenegger in July.

THE HIGHLY CONTESTED QUESTION as to the appropriate candidate for designation as the official state cookie of Pennsylvania remains unresolved seven years after legislation was introduced into the state Senate in 2003 naming the chocolate chip cookie. The lower house refused to agree and introduced its own legislation in favor of the (admittedly lesser known) Nazareth sugar cookie.

IN APRIL 2009, OKLAHOMA governor Brad Henry signed into law recognition of "Do You Realize?" by the Flaming Lips, as the state's official rock song. Oklahoma became only the second state in the union to designate an official state rock song. (Ohio had chosen "Hang on Sloopy" as long ago as 1985.)

OTHER BIZARRE SELECTIONS, WHICH have occupied the time and attention of tax-paid elected representatives, include:

> Official State Aircraft (New Mexico—hot air balloon)
> Official State Artifact (Nevada—Tule duck decoy)
> Official State Bat (Virginia—Virginia big-eared bat)

Official State Bean (Massachusetts—baked navy bean)

Official State Bread (South Dakota—fry bread)

Official State Cantata (Connecticut—The Nutmeg, "Homeland of Liberty" by S. L. Ralph)

Official State Carnivorous Plant (North Carolina—Venus flytrap)

Official State Cartoon Character (Oklahoma—Gusty)

Official State Christmas Tree (North Carolina—Fraser fir)

Official State Cookie (Massachusetts—chocolate chip cookie)

Official State Cooking Implement (Texas—Dutch oven)

Official State Cooking Pot (Utah—Dutch oven)

Official State Covered Bridge (Kentucky—Switzer covered bridge, Franklin County)

Official State Dessert (Maine—Smith Island cake; Missouri—ice cream cone)

Official State Dinosaur (Maryland—Astrodon johnstoni)

Official State Doughnut (Louisiana—beignet)

Official State Exercise (Maine—walking)

Official State Grape (Missouri—Norton/Cynthiana grape)

Official State Hospitality Beverage (South Carolina—tea)

Official State Lullaby (Montana—"Montana Lullaby" by Overcast/Gustafson)

Official State Macroinvertebrate (Delaware—stonefly)

Official State Meal (Oklahoma—cornbread, barbecue pork, okra, squash)

Official State Meat Pie (Louisiana—Natchitoches meat pie)

Official State Molecule (proposed, 2010) (Texas—Buckyball)

Official State Muffin (Massachusetts—corn muffin)

Official State Mushroom (Minnesota—morel mushroom)

Official State Neckware (Arizona—bola tie)

Official State Pepper (Texas—jalapeño)

Official State Percussive Musical Instrument (Oklahoma—drum)

Official State Pie (Florida—key lime pie)

Official State Prepared Food (Georgia—grits)

Official State Quilt (Alabama—Pine Burr Quilt)

Official State Raptor (Idaho—peregrine falcon)

Official State Snack Food (Illinois—popcorn)

Official State Spider (South Carolina—Carolina wolf spider)

Official State Steam Locomotive (Kentucky—Old 152)

Official State Toy (Mississippi—teddy bear)

Official State Troubador (Connecticut—Lara Herscovitch, 2009 & 2010)

 THE KENTUCKY ASSEMBLY FAILED to pass its budget on time in its 2004 session but did devote hours to debating and approving a law to prevent humans and animals being buried in the same cemetery.

FROM THE HISTORY BOOKS

The very first meeting of the U.S. Congress, due to take place in New York, the temporary capital, on March 4, 1789, had to be postponed because not enough legislators had turned up. Only 8 out of the 22 senators and 13 of the 59 representatives had managed to make it. It took a further month, until April 6, before a quorum had been mustered.

A CURIOUS EARLY VICTORIAN trade development was the importation of ice from Norway, used for catering, food preservation, and medical purposes. According to an undated tale in a nineteenth-century collection of political anecdotes, the first consignment into Britain came up against an administrative conundrum, there not being a classification in the Customs House schedule for ice. An application was made to the Treasury, which the Treasury referred on to the Board of Trade. After some delay, it was decided that ice should be entered as "dry goods," but by the time this resolution of the dilemma had been reached and conveyed back to the docking agents, the whole cargo had melted.

4

BEHAVING BADLY: POLITICIANS

We saw in the last chapter how normal governmental duties can nevertheless produce curious outcomes. These are nothing compared to the occasions when elected members choose to flout expected standards, whether it is the exploiting of often quaint rules of procedure for political advantage or crudely breaching the norms of behavior.

EXTREMES OF DEBATE

The head of the Kwa-Zulu homeland, Chief Mangosuthu Buthelezi, set a world record for political loquacity when he opened his Parliament in 1993. His speech setting out the government's policy for the year ran to 427 pages. It took him 18 days to deliver it. Starting on March 12, he had reached the end of the "introductory overview" after six days (and 145 pages). He spoke every weekday, giving legislators the weekend off. The undertaking was not helped by the need to translate parts rendered in Zulu into English and vice versa. He concluded on March 30, when exhausted parliamentarians reportedly leaped to their feet in acclaim. Every member had been required to be present throughout, unless they had urgent business, in which case a deputy had to take their place.

THE SHORTEST SITTING OF a parliamentary committee is believed to be the standing committee meeting in December 1990 to debate an order amending drugs legislation. Conservative government members turned out in full, expecting a prolonged and heated confrontation. To their surprise, not one member of the Opposition arrived. The committee considered the evidence in only 24 seconds. Home Office minister John Patten said it was "a world, not to say intergalactic, record."

GO SLOWS

 The filibuster—the art of excessively prolonging a speech in order to disrupt the proceedings of a law-making body—has produced down the years some extreme examples both of political commitment and physical stamina.

THE LONGEST FILIBUSTER ON record was perpetrated in the U.S. Congress by crusty South Carolina senator Strom Thurmond in 1957, when he spoke uninterrupted for 24 hours and 18 minutes opposing civil rights legislation for African Americans. In doing so, he narrowly beat the existing record set by Wayne Morse, an Independent senator from Oregon, who had held the floor for 22 hours and 26 minutes in 1953 protesting against plans to award states rights over their offshore waters for oil exploration.

NEXT IN THE LINE of honor for this dubious practice appears to be the speech delivered in Ontario's Legislative Assembly in Canada in 1990 by Peter Kormos. He had conducted an eccentric one-man campaign against reform of the car insurance laws. As the sitting on April 26 appeared to be drawing to a welcome 6 p.m. close, he rose and launched into his usual speech—he did not sit down again until 11:00 the next morning, an uninterrupted 17 hours. He enlivened the marathon by giving out the premier's home telephone number and urging people to call it, and offered prizes to those who phoned their support. Over 700 responded. The government hailed the exercise as pointless—as indeed it was. Two weeks later, the new car insurance regulations passed unaltered.

Radical MP Massimo Teodori set an Italian filibuster record in February 1981 when he spoke nonstop in the Chamber of Deputies for 16 hours and 5 minutes protesting against a proposed law giving police powers to detain terrorist suspects for 48 hours without their lawyers. As he made his attempt, the speaker of the chamber was required to observe him through binoculars to ensure he kept within the rules. Teodori was not allowed to lean against his desk for support, and the only refreshment he was allowed was cold water. His party colleagues were suspected of managing to smuggle cups of cappuccino to him. At one point, supporters also provoked Communist deputies into making an intervention. During the interruption, Teodori was able to snaffle an orange.

During a bitter interparty dispute that paralyzed the Alabama Senate for nearly a month in the spring of 1999, Democrat members tried to strip powers from Steve Windom, the state's first Republican lieutenant governor of the twentieth century and speaker of the Senate. Over one-third of the Senate's entire sitting days were lost by a Democrat boycott of proceedings, which prevented any legislation passing.

They then opted for holding marathon sessions in an

attempt to force Windom to leave his chair for a comfort break, at which point they planned to use his absence to vote through their reforms. Determined not to risk leaving his seat, Windom maintained his place uninterrupted for 29 hours. At one point, he was captured on film surreptitiously urinating into a jug hidden under his desk to avoid absenting himself. Commenting afterward on his resistance, he said, "It took guts—and a bladder of steel." The local newspaper, the *Birmingham News*, took a more jaundiced view, editorializing on the politicians' antics that "they have simply gone crazy." Members of the House of Representatives, embarrassed by their upper house colleagues, wore lapel buttons declaring, "I'm in the House. I work."

IRENE SMITH, A CITY councilor in St. Louis, Missouri, was forced to relieve herself in a wastepaper bin in the middle of her filibuster in 2001 protesting proposed changes to district electoral boundaries that would cost her her own seat. The speaker refused to suspend the sitting to allow her a comfort break, so her colleagues gathered round, concealed her with a quilt, and enabled her to "alleviate" herself as she later described it. She was later threatened with prosecution for urinating in public but the charge was dropped.

CONTROVERSIAL PLANS IN JUNE 1992 to commit troops over-seas for the first time since the Second World War led to Japanese parliamentarians resorting to their own unique filibuster tactic. Members of the lower house, where votes are conducted by proceeding to a ballot box in the middle of the chamber, adopted the "ox-walk" to prolong each vote on the proposals. Provided the member continues to advance toward the box, they remain within the rules. Those obstructing the government's plans shuffled infi-nitely slowly, fraction of an inch by fraction of an inch. They managed to stretch out the debate for three uninter-rupted days.

THE TEXAS HOUSE OF Representatives was brought to a standstill for five days in May 2003 when nearly all the Democrat members mounted a novel ploy to thwart their governing Republican opponents from passing changes to the electoral boundaries. Described as "brazen ger-rymandering," the plans would have created seats that would join far-flung parts of the state together to benefit Republican representation in the U.S. Congress. One dis-trict was to be 500 miles long, with others narrowing in places to less than a mile wide before ballooning to take in Republican voters.

With 100 members of the 150-seat legislature required to be present for a quorum to conduct business and aware that, under Texas law, state troopers were empowered to compel attendance by force, 51 Democrat members sabotaged the session by fleeing out of the state just before the crucial vote and holing themselves up in a motel just over the border in Oklahoma. Beyond the reach of Texas Rangers, the House authorities were reduced to issuing arrest warrants for the missing legislators. In return, the Democrats vowed not to return until the controversial law was dropped.

They stayed away until a parliamentary deadline passed that killed the legislation. More than 300 other pieces of planned legislation were also lost as a result of the boycott.

The peace was short-lived, however. Two months later, when the proposals were relaunched, this time in the state's upper house, most of the Democrat senators pulled a similar stunt, flying off to New Mexico to ambush the two-thirds majority needed to pass the law. They stayed away for six weeks before the protest lapsed. By mid-October, the measure had finally passed into law.

A Supreme Court ruling in 2006 later endorsed states' rights to "redistrict" their boundaries how and whenever they liked.

WITH FRIENDS LIKE THESE

For notoriety in political actions, the Texas legislature has a long track record. In 1971, Tom Moore Jr., a representative from Waco, set out to demonstrate his concern that few of his fellow members of the House of Representatives actually paid attention to the resolutions they were passing. He introduced a motion to honor Albert DeSalvo for his pioneering work in population control. DeSalvo was better known as the Boston Strangler, who had murdered 13 women in the Massachusetts city in the early 1960s.

The citation lauded DeSalvo's "dedication and devotion to his work" that has enabled the weak and lonely throughout the nation to achieve and maintain a new degree of concern for their future...He has been officially recognized by the state of Massachusetts for his noted activities and unconventional technique involving population control and applied psychology." The motion passed unanimously.

CONTRIBUTING IN THEIR OWN WAY

The shortest ever speech in the British Parliament is thought to be Lord Mishcon's contribution in May 1985, proposing a clause be added to a piece of environmental legislation that would require environment authorities to report annually on their performance. He simply rose and said, "Why not?"

BARON TREVOR, A CONSERVATIVE peer, made his first speech in the House of Lords in May 1993, 43 years after entering the House. His diffidence was by no means unique. Lord Cullen of Ashbourne, who succeeded to his title in 1932, waited 10 years before taking his seat in the Lords and another 30 before uttering his first speech. Lord Shaughnessy took his seat six weeks before taking part in the Normandy landings in 1944. He then did not make his maiden speech until 1986. The usual reason for these long silences was nonattendance. Perhaps the record for turning up and still not taking part is that of the Earl of Romney, who keenly attended debates but did not utter a single word from his inauguration in 1974 until the demise of the hereditary peers 25 years later.

FRANK MAGUIRE WAS MP for Fermanagh and South Tyrone for seven years between 1974 and his death in 1981. During that time, he visited Westminster infrequently, never actually spoke in the House, and never asked a question. Known as "the Invisible Man," his chief claim to fame was his abstention in the March 1979 no-confidence debate that the Labor government of James Callaghan lost—by one vote—precipitating the general election that brought Margaret Thatcher to power.

PARLIAMENTARY APES

During a late-night transportation debate in the House of Lords in 1985, Lord Carmichael, an opposition peer, spoke unusually slowly. Afterward, he confessed that the whips had told him to string out his speech to keep the debate going until 10:40. At that point, according to House rules, the doorkeepers and other support staff qualified for free taxis home.

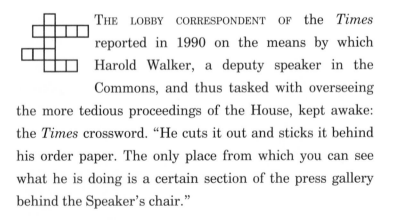 THE LOBBY CORRESPONDENT OF the *Times* reported in 1990 on the means by which Harold Walker, a deputy speaker in the Commons, and thus tasked with overseeing the more tedious proceedings of the House, kept awake: the *Times* crossword. "He cuts it out and sticks it behind his order paper. The only place from which you can see what he is doing is a certain section of the press gallery behind the Speaker's chair."

JIM WEST, U.S. SENATOR from Washington State, proposed to his girlfriend in the middle of a 1990 speech in the Senate.

The bride-to-be, sitting in the gallery, hurried down to the floor, and the couple stood for several minutes in front of the podium while his colleagues applauded.

EXTREMIST MP FILIPPO BERSELLI was ejected from the Italian Chamber of Deputies during a rowdy debate in the summer of 1989 on the problems facing the country's beaches after an invasion of slimy algae had devastated much of Italy's Adriatic coastline and ruined the season's tourism. He made his point by taking off his shoes and socks and standing in the middle of the chamber in a bowl of the polluted sea water, shouting accusations of government inaction.

TO ADDRESS FINLAND'S ALARMINGLY worsening divorce rate, eccentric television star and Social Democrat member of Parliament, Tommy Tabermann, introduced a bill in April 2008 that would require the Finnish state to provide a week's paid holiday annually to every worker for the sole use of shoring up their personal relationships. It has yet to be passed into law.

FOR THREE MONTHS IN 2002, Labor MP Austin Mitchell, who represented the fishing port of Grimsby, legally changed his name to Austin Haddock to promote his constituency's industry. He adopted the new moniker as "a fun way of getting some more publicity for the seafood cause," he said. His wife Linda was reported to be contemplating changing her name to Chips. In December, he announced his intention to revert to Mitchell, saying rather deflatedly that "I didn't get a single letter of thanks" for the stunt.

EVEN AN EVENT AS solemn as the election of a national president became mired in trickery when Italian members of Parliament voted in 1992. A ballot of the MPs had to be rerun when officials discovered that some members had taken more than a single voting paper and cast multiple votes for their candidate. Builders had to construct a voting booth in the chamber overnight, and the politicians had to be processed individually to cast their votes, being handed a single voting slip as they went.

WHEN THE WHEELS COME OFF

In June 1982, proceedings of the French National Assembly descended into chaos when a controversial bill on immigration was sabotaged by opponents. The measure would allow trade unions to carry on negotiations in the languages of the immigrant workforce (mainly Portuguese, Arabic, and Serbo-Croat). Members opposed to the legislation began to conduct the debate in a range of languages to demonstrate the anarchy that would result. The shorthand recorders coped with German and Spanish but sent urgent messages to the chair when one member began speaking in an obscure language from Chad. The prospect of a string of further unfamiliar African and Caribbean tongues was too much. The speaker announced that only those contributions made in French would be taken down for posterity. That was enough to call the protest off.

OTTO AROSOMENA GOMEZ, AN Ecuadorian congressman and former president of the country, shot and wounded two colleagues when a debate in the national assembly turned heated in October 1980.

FRENCH MP JEAN LASSALLE interrupted proceedings of the National Assembly in June 2003 to protest about the relocation of a police station in his constituency by singing during question time. Lassalle, from the Pyrenees, performed a traditional folk song in local dialect and, despite repeated calls to order by the assembly chair, managed to get to the end. He said it had been the only way to draw attention to his complaint.

COLOMBIAN MP LUIS EDUARDO Diaz was suspended by his national parliament in September 2003 for bringing out a rubber dildo during a debate as part of his campaign for sterilization of poor people to cut unwanted births. He left the dildo on the desk of the health minister after complaints about his "disrespect" for Parliament. "A rubber penis is not something that should be brought to Parliament," said a fellow MP. Suspended for five sessions, his antics appeared to have backfired. Rather than take notice of his controversial ideas, most members seemed distracted by the sex toy. One said, "I guess we got so focused on the rubber penis we didn't even pay attention to what he was saying."

THE SWEDISH PARLIAMENT WAS interrupted in 1985 by women protestors in the public gallery who rained down copies of pornographic magazines on MPs who had approved the opening of a sex supermarket in Stockholm. Reporters remarked on the number of copies that were secreted away by members "for research."

BEHAVIOR UNBECOMING

When the Israeli parliamentary committee on science held hearings on the new wonder drug for impotence, Viagra, in June 1998, four of the eight tablets exhibited by doctors giving evidence disappeared during a break in the meeting.

TAIWAN'S PARLIAMENT HAS EARNED a reputation over the last two decades as the world's rowdiest chamber. It started right at the beginning. The opening session of the first Taiwanese Parliament to have a majority of directly elected MPs ended in violence in 1990 after a filibuster by the opposition stopped the prime minister from making his inaugural address. The speaker finally called proceedings to a halt when opposition member Wang Tzung-sung squirted him with a water pistol.

Two years later, the same Parliament suffered 10 days of turmoil during a dispute over a controversial nuclear power plant. Trouble started when an opposition deputy began taking photographs of fellow deputies voting in favor, leading to scuffles and fist fights. Officials estimated the disruption had cost 50 million Taiwan dollars (about $1.7 million) in lost time. The cost of damage to furniture when deputies jumped on it and ripped out microphones had not been calculated.

In 2004, a food fight erupted during a contentious debate over rises in the defense budget. Chu Fong-chih, an opposition deputy, hurled her lunch box of chicken and rice at Chen Tsung-yi, a legislator from the ruling Democratic Progressive Party. Chen responded by flinging his own lunch box at her.

INDIA'S LOWER HOUSE, THE Lok Sabha, runs Taiwan a close second for its ingrained unruliness and, in the favorite description of Indian journalists, its "uproariness." A re-write of the members' code of conduct manual in 1992 found it necessary to remind MPs that it was out of order to knit in the House, carry hats or walking sticks, or read any material unconnected with the business at hand. Carrying arms and ammunition was prohibited; neither could an MP "take shelter within the precincts of Parliament House if he knows he is wanted by the police authorities outside." The latter provision appeared entirely necessary, as estimates in 1996 were that of the 545-seat House returned in that year's election, 27 had criminal records; of the 2009 intake, 153—nearly a third of the entire House—had criminal charges against them, including 9 ministers. In the case of 15 MPs, it was for murder.

THREE SPANISH MPs FROM the ruling Popular Party were fined by their party authorities when they were caught looking at a pornographic website on a laptop while sitting in the parliamentary chamber attending a debate…on the evils of domestic violence against women.

Miguel Perez-Huysmans, the owner of the laptop, was also forced to resign as leader of the party's youth wing. He was fined $960; his two colleagues, $480 each.

A bid to ban laptops in the chamber was said, however, to be unlikely to succeed, as most observers agreed that MPs had little else to do when attending formal debates. Party management of the business of the Spanish Parliament had become so strictly controlled that the expression of personal views was discouraged, with votes being cast by managers on behalf of the whole party rather than by individual members. Real debate had all but disappeared, leaving idle and underoccupied MPs to their own devices for much of the time.

A NUMBER OF CONSERVATIVE members of the European Parliament were censured in 2003 for distributing "sexist" photographs among colleagues to enliven boring committee meetings. Running a mock "Man of the Year" competition, the organizers invited fellow MEPs to judge pictures showing men demeaning their womenfolk. They included a farmer transporting his wife in a cage attached to his tractor and a man walking alongside his partner who was carrying a huge parcel of firewood. The winner was allegedly a picture of a husband genteelly carrying a six-pack of beer while holding hands with a woman struggling with a full crate of bottles.

MEMBERS OF THE U.S. Congress cannily secured themselves a pay rise in 1987 while being able to tell their constituents that they had voted against it. The skillful maneuver was made possible because President Reagan had decided to agree to 15 percent salary increases for both the Senate and House of Representatives, to come into force unless Congress voted against them within 30 days.

Congressional representatives allowed the deadline to pass, and then took a vote formally rejecting the pay raise once it was impossible to stop it coming into force. They thus achieved the best of both worlds.

ORDER, ORDER!

As if human occupants are not troublesome enough, India's legislature suffers from a unique hardship—monkeys. Hundreds live in the precincts of the Parliament building, and are notorious for entering MPs' offices, including the prime minister's secretariat, attacking staff and destroying official papers. Any attempt to eradicate the menace is routinely blocked by Hindu members, for whom the religious connection to the god Hanuman, who won battles by leading an army of monkeys, is revered.

MORE SERENE PROBLEMS CONFRONTED the Swaziland Senate during the budget debate in 1991. A member pointed out to the speaker that others in the chamber appeared to be asleep. The speaker refused to intervene, officially ruling that they could be "concentrating deeply on communicating with their ancestors." If this was the case, and they were suddenly disturbed, they could die from shock.

FACING SIMILAR PROBLEMS, IN 1996 the Thai Parliament found the solution to members dozing: the authorities installed uncomfortable, low-backed chairs that made it impossible to lounge.

THE SPEAKER OF THE New Zealand Parliament, Jonathan Hunt, introduced in November 1999 a soccer-style yellow and red card system to maintain order in his House.

ATTEMPTS TO BAN KNITTING in the New Zealand Parliament failed in 2002. Opposition members were infuriated when the junior minister for commerce, Judith Tizard, got out her knitting on the government bench during a debate involving her ministry. Citing arrogance and disrespect for the House, they sought to have the speaker rule the practice out of order. But to their dismay, Speaker Jonathan Hunt ruled that knitting was not prohibited in the chamber, although it would not be allowed from the seats occupied by ministers.

THE INTRODUCTION OF TELEVISION into debating chambers has, according to some observers, harmed the spontaneity of proceedings in many parliaments. For others, it gives a warts-and-all portrayal of the people's representatives. In 2007, as election fever was rising, Australian viewers were treated to images, thought to date from eight years earlier, of Kevin Rudd, their future prime minister, then a lowly Opposition backbencher, being caught in the background as a member of his party's front bench droned on at the dispatch box, cleaning out his ear with his finger and eating the resulting earwax.

FROM THE HISTORY BOOKS

At the first sitting of the Arkansas House of Representatives in 1837, Speaker of the House John Wilson became enraged by an amendment moved by Representative J. J. Anthony that he deemed to be intended to slight his integrity. When Anthony refused to back down and return to his seat, Wilson descended from the speaker's chair, drew his Bowie knife, and stabbed Anthony on the floor of the House. He died within minutes. Although expelled from office pending trial, he was later acquitted by a jury, which ruled the murder was "excusable homicide." Wilson later won reelection back to the House. The Arkansas chamber is said to be haunted to this day.

In 1584, a member of the public is recorded as having wandered into the chamber of the House of Commons and sat for two hours before being recognized as an intruder. On February 27, 1771, the *Parliamentary Journal* records that a member of the public was admonished by the speaker after he had entered the division lobby and taken part in a vote. Thomas Hunt claimed he had taken part on several votes on previous occasions.

A dog is recorded as having found its way into the debating chamber during Lord North's premiership (1770–82) and interrupted his speech by its loud barking. The records also show that on May 14, 1605, "a strange spaniel, of mouse-color, came into the House."

ESSAYIST AND PIONEER JOURNALIST Joseph Addison sat in the House of Commons representing Malmesbury for 11 years from 1708 until his death in 1719 but never uttered a word in debate because of shyness. Despite this, he served as secretary to the lord lieutenant of Ireland, became a commissioner of trade, chief secretary for Ireland, and finally, two years before he died, secretary of state for the Southern Department, a forerunner of the foreign secretaryship—all without ever speaking in Parliament.

Future prime minister Lord Bute, who became premier in 1762, sat in Parliament for two months short of 25 years without uttering a word in debate. He made his maiden speech just three months before becoming prime minister.

The Duke of Portland managed to become prime minister in 1783 without having spoken in the House at all. He made his first contribution six days after taking the top office. He had held ministerial office as early as 1765.

Despite penning a million and a half words in his magisterial six-volume *The History of the Decline and Fall of the Roman Empire*, Edward Gibbon sat for eight years as a member of Parliament between 1774 and 1782 and did not utter a single word in debate.

THE U.S. SENATE FAMOUSLY failed to endorse the post-First World War Treaty of Versailles, which created the League of Nations, the brainchild of their own president, Woodrow Wilson. In opposing approval the chief antagonist, Massachusetts senator Henry Cabot Lodge, who chaired the Foreign Relations Committee, read the entire 264-page treaty aloud as part of a filibuster to draw out the debate.

MANY WOULD HAVE PREFERRED it if the same affliction applied to eighteenth-century member David Hartley. So notorious was he for treating the House to long, turgid speeches that he became widely known as "the dinner bell." As soon as he rose, it was safe to leave the chamber and go to dinner. Charles Jenkinson, father of future prime minister Lord Liverpool, took advantage of this in 1779 when Hartley had risen at about five o'clock on a summer's evening. It being "generally understood that he would continue a long time on his legs, [Jenkinson] profited by the occasion to breathe some country air. He walked, therefore, from the House to his residence in Parliament Street; from whence, mounting his horse, he rode to a place...some miles out of town. There he dined, he sent his servant to the House to inquire who had spoken...and when a division might be expected. The footman brought back the answer that Mr. Hartley continued still speaking." When Jenkinson returned to the chamber at about 9 p.m. Hartley was still on his feet "regardless of the general impatience or of the profound repose into which the majority of his hearers were sunk."

SIR JOHN TREVOR, SPEAKER of the House of Commons in 1685 and again from 1690 to 1695, had one of the most unfortunate afflictions for his office. He was severely cross-eyed. Parliamentary legend tells of many occasions when confusion reigned as more than one member of Parliament thought he had received the speaker's nod to address the House next. As a direct result of the problems caused, speakers introduced the practice, still in use today, of calling out the name of the member selected to speak next instead of relying on the silent nod.

THE SHORTCOMINGS OF CHARLES Wolfran Cornwall, elected speaker in late 1780, were entirely self-inflicted. He had the habit, in the words of a contemporary observer, of keeping a large pot of beer "constantly at hand, from which he imbibed large quantities" during debates, which "considerably detracted from the dignity of his office." The drunk speaker often fell asleep, which "on more than one occasion is said to have caused considerable inconvenience to the House." Remarkably, he remained speaker for over 8 years, dying in office in January 1789.

JOSEPH BROTHERTON, MP FOR Salford from 1832 until his sudden death in 1857, had a religious obsession that all good Christians should go to bed before midnight. That the House of Commons regularly sat into the early hours was deeply offensive to him and, for over 20 years, every night that the Commons was sitting he would rise in his place on the stroke of twelve and formally move that the House adjourn. He rarely succeeded, but he never stopped trying.

WOMEN WERE BANNED FROM observing the House of Commons for over 60 years after attending debates became a society occasion in the later eighteenth century. It reached a notorious crescendo in February 1778 when, for a major debate on the state of the nation, a flock of society ladies occupied all the seats in the public gallery. When complaints were made to the speaker and they were ordered to leave, the women created two hours of mayhem in their refusal. A formal ban was quickly introduced, and was lifted only in 1842 when, seven years after the matter was reraised, a special ladies gallery was built. To guard against a concern that male MPs might be influenced by the sight of females while they spoke, women were delicately obscured behind an ornate grille so that their presence could not be seen from the chamber below. They were thrown out again in 1888 because of the rising women's suffrage campaign that had led to frequent interruptions of debates. When they were allowed back in 1909, all women visitors had to sign a written declaration promising to behave. The grilles were not removed until 1918.

THERE HAS BEEN ONE occasion when, for five months, a prime minister of another country sat as a member of the House of Commons. Maltese-born Sir Gerald Strickland set up and led the Constitutional Party as the main opposition force in Malta from 1921 to 1927. At the same time, he occupied a seat at Westminster, having won Lancaster for the Conservatives in 1924. In August 1927, he became prime minister of Malta. He continued to sit in London too until the principle was questioned by other MPs. The delicate situation was resolved by Strickland being made a peer in the New Year's Honors List of 1928. He remained prime minister of Malta until 1932.

5

OFFICE AND RESPONSIBILITY: GOVERNMENT

The responsibilities of office take governments down many strange avenues. Some are of their choosing and others are forced on them by events. Picking one's way through the minefield is not always straightforward. What's clear is that the machinery of government often runs far from smoothly.

AFFAIRS OF STATE

As part of its antipoverty strategy in the 1980s, the Bangladesh government subsidized the cost of gas to householders by levying a flat charge of $1.60 per month. It later found that users were keeping their cookers alight all day because it saved on the cost of buying matches. The ill-fated policy was thought to have cost the cash-strapped economy millions of dollars in wasted gas.

WHEN REWRITING ITS CONSTITUTION in 1978 after 4 military coups in 10 years, Nigerian lawmakers inserted a clause formally making coups d'état illegal. In the 15 years that followed, there were 3 more.

THE BRITISH MINISTRY OF Defense put up for sale the aircraft carrier Hermes in 1985. It received an early expression of interest from an 8-year-old schoolboy who offered $24 plus $12 in gift tokens. The MoD declined the bid, saying it couldn't accept tokens.

THE CANADIAN PROVINCE OF Manitoba was plunged into chaos in June 1985 when the nation's Supreme Court ruled that all its laws passed over the previous 95 years were invalid, and "of no force or effect." Legislators had passed an act in 1890 declaring English to be the only official language, in contravention of the Canadian constitution, which gave equal status to French. The issue had languished in the prairie province because of the lack of French influence. Politicians faced the task of translating an estimated 4,500 laws and up to 30,000 regulations. It took until 1990 to reenact them all.

THE PHILIPPINE PARLIAMENT VOTED to reintroduce the death penalty in 1993, specifying in the law that execution had to be by electric chair until a gas chamber had been built. A year later, the director of the Bureau of Corrections officially wrote to senators complaining that he had accumulated 54 inmates on death row, none of which he could execute because the gas chamber had been stalled by a safety inspector who had discovered that the brickwork leaked gas and could be "a public health hazard." The country's only electric chair had been destroyed in an accident years earlier.

Clearly neither problem was solved: when the first execution eventually took place five years later in 1999, it was by lethal injection.

DURING A PARTICULARLY NERVY stage of the Iran-Iraq war in 1982, Iraqi leader Saddam Hussein sought to strengthen morale by publicizing examples of heroic devotion to the cause. The most outlandish claim reported was of a charge on the battlefield led by 27 men—all blind. And after a spate of surrenders in 1986, the Iraqi military command reportedly halted the supply of white underwear to front-line troops.

THE FRENCH GOVERNMENT AGENCY set up in 2009 to police Internet piracy, illegal downloading, and copyright theft issues had to apologize when it was discovered to be using a copyrighted logo without permission. The owner of the logo, which had been copied from France Telecom, was at the time of writing threatening legal action.

IN JULY 1982, THE ruling crown prince of the tiny Alpine state of Liechtenstein had to bail out his government when it discovered it had no law against the sale of narcotic drugs. Prince Franz Josef used his emergency powers to declare that the laws of neighboring Switzerland on the matter had immediate effect.

THE TASMANIAN GOVERNMENT FOUND itself unable to publish its list of censored publications in 1977 because the state's attorney general advised that doing so would contravene the government's own obscenity laws.

IN 2006, THE UK government inadvertently repealed its law that made it an offense to use a forged passport. Due to a mix-up over the timing of bringing into force the new Identity Cards Act, ministers found they had repealed the old law relating to passports without introducing the new provisions. Several courts around the country were forced to dismiss cases, as it was technically no longer illegal to use a false passport. The following month, the government hastily issued the necessary statutory instrument to re-establish the offense.

THE NEW MINORITY CONSERVATIVE Canadian government elected in January 2006 did not go out of its way to endear itself to a key segment of the populace when Prime Minister Stephen Harper appointed as junior minister for Francophone affairs, the government post dedicated to maintaining the linguistic interests of French-speaking Canadians, an MP with a distinct disadvantage for the job: he could not speak French. Riling the perennially fragile Anglo-French cultural divide in the country, the appoint-ment of Ted Menzies, an Albertan from the prairies of cen-tral Canada, caused an outrage when his lack of capacity in French was disclosed. He quickly committed himself to language lessons three times a week and to "total immer-sion" in Quebec in his free time. Perhaps fortuitously for both parties, by October 2007 he had moved on.

THE SOUTH AFRICAN GOVERNMENT laid on a spectacu-lar public relations show in February 1988 to mark the 500th anniversary of the landing of Portuguese explorer Bartholomew Dias, the first European to discover the Cape of Good Hope and the southern sea route to the Indies. A reenactment of the landing and the first encounter with Hottentot natives was held at the site of the landfall in Mossel Bay, attended by President Botha, his cabinet, and 8,000 African and overseas dignitaries. The strictures of apartheid caused one small problem, however. To portray the native reception committee, the organizers had to make do with six white actors dressed in loincloths, wearing fuzzy wigs, and liberally doused with walnut juice. The beach they were on was officially designated as whites only. According to reports, few in the audience appeared to notice the deception.

IN PUBLIC INTEREST

In the 1970s, the Dutch government required that all television advertisements for sweets show a toothbrush at least one-tenth the height of the screen throughout the commercial.

To MAINTAIN THE STANDARDS expected in the upmarket Providencia neighborhood of Chile's capital, Santiago, local municipal councilors introduced a bylaw requiring every resident of private property to keep a grass patch in the street immediately outside their front gate. In April 2002, Gloria

Cisternas, a mother of four, was sentenced to seven days in jail for refusing to lay turf outside her house. She spent two days incarcerated before a public outcry over the case forced the country's president to get involved. The conviction was later quashed.

IN THE FACE OF an increase in crime, the city council in the small U.S. town of Kennesaw, Georgia, enacted a municipal ordinance in May 1982 making ownership of a firearm compulsory for every head of household. Anyone not having a gun and ammunition faced a $200 fine and 60 days in jail. The law exempted the disabled, householders with religious objections, and, perhaps wisely, convicted felons. The law is still in force.

CITY COUNCILORS IN SANTA Monica, California, passed a bylaw in November 1991 allowing women to use men's public toilets if the line for theirs was more than three strong, on the grounds that, as men rarely had to queue, doing so breached rights under sex discrimination legislation.

SAN FRANCISCO'S GOVERNING BODY, the Board of Supervisors, voted in May 2000 to outlaw discrimination on the grounds of size. A "fat acceptance" ordinance was passed unanimously that added to a long list of antidiscrimination measures. City laws already banned discrimination on the grounds of race, color, religion, age, ancestry, sex, sexual orientation, disability, place of birth, and gender identity (to protect transsexuals).

President of the board, Tom Ammiano, claimed the move was needed because "people are being denied employment, housing, bank loans on the grounds that they are overweight." The new legislation decreed that "weight may not be used as a measure of health, fitness, endurance, flexibility, strength of character, or self-control." The only employers exempted from the law were the police, fire service, and unionized strip clubs.

From now on, San Francisco's Human Rights Commission was empowered to investigate allegations of discrimination. Among those affected by the rules were cinemas and theaters, who were required to install an adequate supply of extrawide seats, although ticket clerks were not allowed to point out their existence to ticket buyers, as that would be discriminatory.

The self-styled "fat acceptance" movement began in the city in 1999 after a health club advertising for new members ran a billboard campaign depicting an alien with the slogan, "When They Come, They'll Eat the Fat Ones First."

THE U.S. FEDERAL TAX Authority followed suit in 2002 by announcing that obese people could claim tax allowances in future on weight-loss expenses. The Internal Revenue Service ruled that those with medically diagnosed fat problems could deduct the costs of "mitigation, treatment or prevention" of their condition. Observers foresaw definitional difficulties ahead, with questions over whether gym membership or purchases of slimming foods would qualify remaining to be clarified.

THE MAYOR OF THE Italian coastal resort of Diano Marina proposed in the summer of 1995 that only slim and beautiful women should be allowed to wear bikinis in his town. Andrea Guglieri was reported by Turin's *La Stampa* newspaper as declaring, "I don't want people who don't have good physiques walking the streets in their swimming costumes." The mayor had commissioned a professor of aesthetics from the University of Milan to draw up a 10-point guide to help officials decide who was and was not beautiful.

UNTIL THE MID-1980S, POLITICIANS in Belgium dictated what parents could call their children. The choice could be made only from an official register of 1,500 accepted monikers dating from the Napoleonic era. The government announced its intention to abolish the list in 1984. In future, families would have free choice except for names that were judged "absurd, shocking, or ridiculous."

AFTER THE ISLAMIC REVOLUTION in 1979, the new rulers of Iran imposed strict moral codes for the defense of the nation's females. All buses required segregation, with men traveling on the top deck and women on the bottom.

IN 1973, THE GOVERNMENT of the West African state of Sierra Leone instituted the Medal of the Mosquito, a new award to mark civil and military gallantry. It was named after the insect, according to the announcement, to honor the effect the bug had had on making the country a "white man's graveyard" and preventing Europeans from permanently settling.

SINGAPORE, WHICH HAS BECOME notorious for its authoritarian approach to social engineering, banned chewing gum in 1992, supposedly because of the cost of removing discarded gum from pavements. Suppiah Dhanabalan, foreign minister and minister of culture, gave a little more away when he complained that gum chewing was "obnoxious. All it does is exercise the jaw." Lawmakers imposed a penalty of a year in jail, and a 10,000 Singapore dollar ($8,000) fine for smuggling gum into the country. The ban had to be partially relaxed in 2004 to comply with international trade rules. Citizens, however, were still required to register for permission to acquire gum.

It was not the first antisocial practice to feel the wrath of Singaporean legislators. In 1989, the city-state passed regulations making it an offense not to flush a toilet after use.

THE EASTERN CANADIAN CITY of Halifax, Nova Scotia, introduced what was thought to be a world's first in February 2000—a ban on wearing perfume or scented products in a public place. Intended to prevent illnesses caused by allergies, the bylaw applied to all public locations, including schools, hospitals, and the public transportation system. It covered not only colognes and cosmetics but also scented aftershaves, hairsprays, and deodorants. Stung by nationwide ridicule, the city authorities later replaced the ban with a public relations campaign advocating a "scent-free" environment. It still runs today.

DETROIT CITY COUNCIL INTRODUCED a similar ban for all its employees in March 2010 after a worker managed to win

$100,000 damages in the local courts by complaining that her colleague's perfume affected her breathing. Council staff would be discouraged from wearing scented deodorants, aftershaves, or body lotions. Even air fresheners were on the forbidden list. Observers speculated how long it would be until the city faced its first reverse complaint about a co-worker's unhygienic body odor.

THE OHIO STATE DEPARTMENT of Natural Resources outwitted two environmental protestors in 2001 who staged a week-long sit-in to obstruct the logging of trees in rural Vinton County. Having arrested the pair for trespassing, the department chopped down the two trees they had occupied on the grounds that they contained the fingerprints of the culprits and would be needed for evidence in court. It then billed the protesters $152 for the cost of cutting down the trees.

PENTAGON OFFICIALS REJECTED A Freedom of Information Act request in November 2003 from a press reporter asking to see the Defense Department's internal training video "Freedom of Information Act—the People's Right to Know," a film used to teach bureaucrats how to comply with the act. No reason was given for withholding the film.

Austria's new Social Democrat minister for Women's Affairs, Helga Konrad, announced plans in August 1995 to introduce legislation to force men to do equal amounts of domestic chores as women. Failure to do so would become a ground for divorce. Compulsory courses at "marriage schools" covering housework, child care, wage distribution, and fidelity were envisaged to prepare prospective spouses for their obligations. Konrad also proposed that legally binding prenuptial contracts would be introduced for all marrying couples. Opposition commentators ridiculed the idea as overly intrusive into families' private lives. The proposed law never materialized, and by 1997 Konrad was no longer a minister.

The UK Department of Education spent £50,000 (about $80,000) producing a "Dad Pack" of guidance for fathers in 2006 that, according to critics, contained "astonishingly obvious" advice. It told them how to play with their children ("take them to a playground") as well as suggesting "hide and seek and making paper patterns." It contained a poster with a hundred phrases on how to praise a child, as well as advice on fidelity ("don't have an affair").

France, which had a law limiting parents to names of saints or historical figures, abolished its restrictions only in

1993—mostly. Authorities kept a reserve power to forbid a name if it was judged likely to be against the interests of the child. In 1999, a prosecutor in Besançon invoked the powers to prevent a couple naming their child Zebulon, on the grounds that it was the Gallic version of Zebedee from the children's television series, *The Magic Roundabout*. This was judged to be likely to cause the child "inevitable sarcasm and mockery." Despite the parents' protests that it had an ancient and esteemed Biblical origin, the French authorities prevailed.

LOCAL AUTHORITIES IN JAPAN have powers to vet the suitability of names. In 1993, Tokyo city hall rejected a couple's attempt to register their baby son as Satan. After a six-month battle, the parents gave up and announced he would be called God.

SWEDISH COUPLE SARA LINDENGER and Johan Leisten were banned by the authorities from calling their son Staalman, Swedish for "Superman," in 2003. The government disallowed the registration, saying it would be "unpleasant" for the boy in later life.

ANOTHER SWEDISH COUPLE, UNIDENTIFIED in news reports, managed to have a ban overturned by the Court of Appeal in 2008 after the authorities had tried to stop them naming their son Lego, after the toy brick.

BUREAUCRACY RULES

The U.S. Department of Housing introduced a sophisticated new computer program in 1987 to revamp its methods for assessing entitlements for federal funding across American municipalities. The program evaluated a raft of socioeconomic data to find the neediest places in the country. On the first list churned out of the computer was Beverly Hills, California, possibly the most glamorous and well-endowed community on the planet. Investigations showed that the program had worked correctly. The housing stock of sprawling mansions, built in the Hollywood boom years between the wars, was interpreted as "pre-1940 housing"; the army of retired film stars showed up as a glut of elderly unemployed; and the city's enormous but static wealth was scored as slow growth. Despite the flaws, the department still offered the city $56 million in grants. Graciously, it declined.

THE WASHINGTON-BASED NATIONAL FISH and Wildlife Service changed the identification markings on its bird-tracking tags in 1998 after receiving a letter from an aggrieved camper in Arkansas. The man wrote that he had caught a bird and noticed the tag, inscribed "Wash.Biol.Surv." "I followed the cooking instructions on the leg and I want to tell you it was horrible."

THE U.S. NATIONAL PARKS Service, which is responsible for America's National Historic Landmarks program, conferred the much coveted landmark status on a municipal rubbish dump at Fresno, California, in August 2001. It cited the tip as worthy of recognition for being the oldest sanitary landfill in the country.

A UK HOME OFFICE report on police integrity published in June 1999 condemned leaks from the force, citing them as tantamount to police corruption. Details of the report came as no surprise to journalists. The conclusions had been leaked to a police magazine two weeks earlier.

TRADING STANDARDS OFFICERS IN Crickhowell, Wales, warned the makers of Welsh Dragon Sausages in November 2006 that they risked prosecution, as the labeling could be misleading for customers. The problem appeared to be that the sausages, which were made from pork and chili, failed to mention pork in the title, although it was clearly in the small-print list of ingredients. "I don't think any of our customers actually believe that we use dragon meat," the owner of the business told the press. "This is bureaucracy gone mad." He was forced to include the word "pork" more prominently on the label in the future to escape further action.

DURING POWER SHORTAGES IN the Australian state of New South Wales in 1982, the State Electricity Commission rejected a request from the firm Polly & Sons for exemption from power cuts. The company made the application because of heavy demands for their product. They made candles.

NORTH CAROLINA PASSED LEGISLATION regulating funeral services in July 2001, which included a prohibition against the use of "profanity, indecent, or obscene language" in the presence of a corpse.

ANNOUNCING THE ARRIVAL INTO service in 1986 of its B-1 Lancer, the next generation of nuclear strategic bomber, which is capable of delivering enough nuclear weaponry to destroy half a dozen cities, the U.S. Defense Department was at pains to highlight how the design had catered to environmental concerns. The current official USAF fact sheet states that:

Development of the B-1, from the program's inception, has been in consonance with all Federal environmental laws, executive orders, regulations, and with criteria and standards published by the Environmental Protection Agency. Every effort is being made to minimize the effects of the aircraft on the environment.

The B-1's engines incorporate new technology that makes them among the cleanest and most efficient ever built. Tests indicate that the F101 engine has a combustion efficiency of 99.5 percent and is virtually smokeless...

While specific fuel consumption is classified, the B-1 will use about 25 percent less fuel than the B-52 for the same mission...

Noise levels of the B-1, when its afterburners are not in use, are considerably lower than those of other military aircraft; they compare favorably with the newest commercial aircraft.

BENT ON CLAMPING DOWN on loss of income, Indian State Railways minister Laloo Prasad Yadav, renowned for his publicity seeking, launched a high-profile campaign in 2007 to try to recoup millions of rupees in lost revenue from fare dodgers. It backfired for him personally when two of the first catches were his elderly in-laws, who were both caught in a first-class carriage without tickets and fined 1,800 rupees each.

 THE GOVERNOR OF THE central Russian region of Ulyanovsk launched a campaign to boost the dwindling population in 2005 by declaring September 12 an official "Day of Conception." Sergei Morozov encouraged couples to take the day off to procreate on behalf of the country's future, which had been witnessing alarming population declines since the fall of communism. Women who gave birth exactly nine months later stood a chance of winning prizes, including cash, a television, a car, or even a refrigerator. After three years, statistics showed that the birth rate in June was three times the normal daily average.

DIRE STRAITS

During the economic meltdown of Russia, the government of the autonomous republic of Altai in the center of the country was so strapped for cash in 1998 that it began paying its teachers' salaries in vodka. Eight thousand were paid 15 bottles each. The authorities had originally tried to pay part of the six months' pay arrears with toilet paper—but staff rejected the idea.

Continuing economic hardship in 2001 led to 400 staff in the hospital at Nizhni Novgorod in central Russia being offered bags of manure in lieu of wages. They refused. Senior doctors said they would have to have been given six tons of manure to equate to their monthly salary.

The most celebrated example of workers accepting goods in place of cash was a group of loggers in Archangel in Russia's Arctic north. They were paid in tampons for the whole of 1994.

THE SWEDISH PARLIAMENT'S INTRODUCTION of stringent budget cuts and a ban on overtime in May 2001 led to the head of the national navy announcing that it was cutting back on around-the-clock operations. In the future, it would provide defense services only from 9 a.m. to 5 p.m., Monday to Friday.

THE HEAD OF COLOMBIA'S armed forces, General José Manuel Bonnet, announced desperate measures in October 1997 in the country's 40-year-old war against drug cartels. He broadcast on national television and radio an appeal to all Colombian women to deny sex to drug traffickers, guerrillas, and paramilitaries until they lay down their arms. "I propose a sexual strike until December to demand an end to violence...I see it as a last resort attempt to bring peace to our war-ravaged country." The war is still going on.

TAXING MATTERS

Legislators in Kansas introduced the bizarre require-ment in 1987 for dealers in illegal drugs to pay tax on every packet of narcotics they sell. Under a law that 20 American states have since copied, the state revenue ser-vice sells drug tax stamps that are required to be affixed to every pack of drugs traded. Officials defended the scheme against criticism of double standards by stress-ing that the stamps did not legalize drug dealing, and any trader caught without duly stamped drugs faces not only the drug offenses but tax evasion too. The penalty for not buying the tax stamps is itself five years, along with huge fines for evasion.

Surprisingly, by 2003 nearly $145,000 was being raised in a six-month period on marijuana sales and $305,000 on cocaine and amphetamines. State officials pointed to constitutional protections against self-incrimination that enabled dealers to have anonymity when buying the stamps, and information on stamp sales was protected from being passed on to other law enforcement bodies.

A YEAR AFTER THE Danish Parliament legalized prostitution, the national tax authority ruled in September 2000 that a massage parlor worker was entitled to claim tax relief on her $3,300 breast implants, as they constituted a legitimate business investment to "improve facilities."

THE NORWEGIAN TAX AUTHORITIES were required by their national courts in 2005 to allow striptease clubs to enjoy the same exemption from 25 percent value added tax on entry fees as opera, ballet and theater, ruling that the performance constituted "art."

 BURIED IN ITS 305-PAGE official instructions that the U.S. Internal Revenue Service issues to U.S. taxpayers on how to complete their returns in 2010, a chapter for "other income" has the requirement that "if you receive a bribe, include it in your income" (page 92). For anyone uncertain, there are more details under "illegal activities" on page 94: "Income from illegal activities, such as money from dealing illegal drugs, must be included in your income on Form 1040, line 21, or on schedule C or Schedule C-EZ (Form 1040) if from your self-employment activity." Under "kickbacks" (page 95): "You must include kickbacks, side

commissions, push money, or similar payments you receive in your income." And for the diligent burglar, under "stolen property": "If you steal property, you must report its fair market value in your income in the year you steal it unless in the same year, you return it to its rightful owner."

IN JANUARY 2005, THE Dutch tax authorities, following legal precedents, allowed a convicted bank robber to claim the $2,240 cost of the gun used in the crime as a business expense. He was able to set off the cost against the $7,525 proceeds of the robbery and had his court-imposed fine reduced by that amount. He did have to serve four years in jail.

FACING A BACKLOG OF 38 million rupees ($728,179) in unpaid municipal taxes, the Indian city of Hyderabad inaugurated a novel method of recovering payment in March 2005. The revenue agency hired 10-strong bands of drummers to set up camp outside the homes of nonpayers with orders to maintain nonstop drumming until recalcitrants paid up.

THE IDEA CAUGHT ON. In 2006, the municipal corporation of Patna, the main city of Bihar state, the country's poorest and most backward state, which was managing a collection rate of only 4 percent, went one step further and hired groups of eunuchs, transsexuals, and hermaphrodites to stand outside nonpayers' homes and businesses to humiliate owners into paying up.

WASTE NOT...

Between 1975 and 1988, Wisconsin senator William Proxmire occupied a legendary position in American politics through the monthly publishing of his "Golden Fleece" awards to publicize the most outrageous examples of waste by agencies of the U.S. government. His first award, in March 1975, went to the National Science Foundation for spending $84,000 on finding out why people fall in love. Among the other bizarre uses of taxpayers' dollars, Proxmire rewarded:

- the Head of the Federal Energy Administration for spending $25,000 and 19,000 gallons of fuel in 10 months flying around the country urging businesses and civic groups to economize on energy resources (November 1975)

- the Law Enforcement Assistance Administration for a $27,000 study to determine why inmates want to escape from prison (February 1977)

- the National Endowment for the Humanities for making a $25,000 grant to Arlington County, Virginia, to study why people are rude, cheat, and lie on the local tennis courts (May 1977)

- the Law Enforcement Assistance Administration (again) for developing at a cost of $2 million, and then scrapping, a prototype police car. The vehicle included, among other gadgets, a visual indicator that showed whether or not the siren was on (January 1978)

- the Federal Highway Administration for commissioning a $222,000 study, "Motorist Attitudes Toward Large Trucks" (June 1978)

- the Environmental Protection Agency for spending $1.2 million to preserve a New Jersey sewer as a historical monument, despite being 25 feet underground and having been visited by just two people in 23 years (February 1980)

- the U.S. Coast Guard for wasting $500,000 in starting a computer conversion project that was later abandoned when, after three years, only 7 percent of the work had been completed (April 1980)

- the U.S. Army for spending $6,000 on a 17-page document to instruct military supply managers how to buy foodstuffs (July 1981)

- the U.S. Army for a 13-year, $35 million program on developing a better gas mask, whose product was no better than existing gas masks (May 1982)

- the U.S. Coast Guard (again) for spending $1.1 million on a North Carolina boatyard that then remained empty and unused for a year (July 1983)

- the National Institute of Dental Research for sponsoring a 5-year, $465,000 study on the psychological effect on patients of going to the dentist (April 1984)

- the Federal Crop Insurance Corporation for its $12 million publicity campaign for farmers, a follow-up study of which showed that awareness levels were no higher after the campaign than before (July 1984)

SHORTLY AFTER BECOMING STATE premier of Victoria, Australia, Steve Bracks ordered a study costing the equivalent of $16,810 for advice on how to make his office more efficient. According to press reports in April 2001, the major conclusion provided by the consultants was for him to keep a pad and pencil beside his telephone to take notes during calls.

A UK GOVERNMENT REGULATOR for the railways, the Rail Safety and Standards Board, took two years and spent $800,485 to produce a report that concluded that passengers preferred their trains to run on time and not be overcrowded. Published in May 2009, it found that passengers were likely to be in a "positive emotional state" if trains were punctual and announcements were audible and understandable. In contrast, they were likely to have "negative" attitudes if trains were late and there was no information telling them why.

THE INDIAN STATE GOVERNMENT of Madhya Pradesh approved a scheme in 2004 to pay police officers an extra 30 rupees a month (about 60 cents) if they grew moustaches to give them a more military bearing. Research claimed to show that local people respected officers with moustaches, a traditional sign of virility in India, more readily than those without. A senior official explained, "These men would patrol sensitive pockets in the district employing psychological tactics against criminals...Though thick moustaches have been traditionally associated with bandits dwarfing their victims psychologically, this 'warfare' will be employed against criminals here."

THE ENVIRONMENT DEPARTMENT OF California conducted its 1990 survey of sources of pollution with the intention of it being the most comprehensive scrutiny yet compiled. Its final report included in its list of "sources potentially harmful to health" San Quentin jail—on account of its gas chamber.

LOS ANGELES CITY COUNCIL was discovered in 2005 to have been spending thousands of dollars of taxpayers' money on bottled water for its staff while it was running a $1 million program trying to persuade residents of the city to drink the tap supply provided by the municipality. The Department of Power and Water—the agency managing domestic water provision—was responsible for more than a third of the spending.

SHORTLY AFTER TAKING OFFICE in 1993, U.S. Vice President Al Gore published a 168-page policy document outlining how the new administration would be more efficient than the last. It ended up costing three times as much to produce as it should have because it was printed on expensive ("Grade 1") glossy paper, in color, and sent as a rush printing job over a public holiday. Instead of costing 90 cents a copy to print, the bill turned out at $4, bringing the total expense to over $165,000 instead of the budgeted $55,000. The title of the report was *Creating a Government That Works Better and Costs Less*.

UNDER A CITY ORDINANCE that provides for up to 2 percent of costs of new public buildings to be devoted to art furnishings, San Francisco's new $54 million city jail, which opened in 1994, spent $600,000 on decorative adornments, including a $22,000 60-foot-long, hand-carved jade couch in the reception area, computer-controlled skylights that track the sun at a cost of $64,000, and $70,000 "meditation atriums." The jail, known locally as the "Glamour Slammer," was so over-budget when it was finished that the authorities did not have enough funds left to fully staff the facility.

THE COURT OF ACCOUNTS, France's top spending watchdog, issued an unusually scathing review of the wastage of public money in 1996. It highlighted a 140 million franc (about $28,469,900) airstrip built in Antarctica for French scientists that had been completed in 1993 after seven years' work. The Environment Ministry had immediately banned use of the runway for certain months of the year because it was a breeding ground for penguins and other rare birds. Scientists then discovered that at every other time of year, the weather conditions were too bad for landings. The airport has never been used.

A NEW 16-PAGE CITIZENS' guide on antiterrorism preparation issued by agencies in New York City in November 2003 contained the instruction, "Do not accept packages from strangers; if you find yourself holding a mysterious substance, put it down." Among the other helpful guidance was, "If you encounter radiation, go outside (if you are inside a building) or go inside (if you are outside a building)."

THE U.S. OFFICE OF Economic Opportunity launched a $100,000 contraceptive supply program in deprived areas of Cleveland and Philadelphia in 1971, targeted at promiscuous young males. The scheme amassed a list of 43,000 specific individuals known to local social services, each of whom received letters with vouchers for 12 free condoms. Only 254 of the recipients redeemed their vouchers, putting the cost to the public purse of the condoms at $400 per dozen.

A POLICE STATION IN the Swedish town of Hagfors, on the other hand, was refreshingly prudent with its money: it ordered its first roll of toilet paper in 20 years in 2006, having seen itself through the consequences of a clerical error in 1986 when it ordered 20 pallets of rolls instead of 20 packets. It had been diligently working through the consignment ever since. The downside of the achievement, according to police chief Bjorn Fredlund, was that the paper had all been single ply. "Double ply would have been nice."

IN SAFE HANDS?

IN 1997, the written test for student drivers set by New York State's Department of Motor Vehicles included a multiple-choice question that read: "A 'No Parking' sign at a certain location means…"

CONCERNED BY AN INCREASE in failures in their state tests, the California Department of Motor Vehicles simplified its written exam to a reading age level of 11. Among the multiple-choice questions was "What does a six-sided Stop sign mean?" The most frequent answer in Culver City, Los Angeles, was "slow down to 25 miles per hour."

NEW JERSEY'S CHIEF OF the Division of Alcohol Beverage Control resigned in 1999 after being pulled over by police for drunk driving, John Holl had served in the post for six years, leading a crackdown on alcohol-related crime, including organizing a conference on responsible drinking and increasing police patrols.

MOSCOW CITY AUTHORITIES LAUNCHED a safe-driving campaign in early 2000 by mounting car wrecks on top of poles on some of the city's busiest routes to warn drivers of the perils of speeding. After a month of operation, they claimed the scheme had reduced accidents. It had caused a few too. The dramatic sight of cars suspended above the street had caused motorists to take their eyes off the road and resulted in multiple accidents.

NEW YORK CITY'S BUREAU for At-Risk Children introduced an antidrugs campaign in schools in 1998 using pencils bearing the slogan, "Too Cool to Do Drugs." No one appeared to have thought through the consequences of extended use. Teachers reported that after a few resharpenings, the pencils carried the message, "Cool to Do Drugs," and later, simply "Do Drugs." The scheme was abandoned.

Two dozen U.S. soldiers who were returned from service in Iraq in 2008 suffering from shell shock were sent by Army officials for rehabilitation at Fort Benning on the Georgia-Alabama border, home to one of America's largest complex of firing ranges. The soldiers later complained that the almost constant gunfire from the base's 67 live firing ranges was not assisting their recovery. Brigadier Gary Cheek, director of the army's Warrior Care and Transition Office responded to media enquiries by saying, "I can see how that would be a problem. It's something we haven't considered."

Residents of Hartford, Connecticut, were spared serving on federal grand juries for three years in the mid-1980s because a state computer system had registered all citizens of the city as being dead. When administrators, noticing the curious absence of Hartford addresses appearing on juries, reviewed the system they discovered that data had been entered in the wrong column of the database, having the effect that the "d" of the city's name slipped over into the next column. There, the letter was recognized by the computer system as signifying the nominee had died.

THE U.S. DEPARTMENT OF Justice advertised in 2010 for new attorneys to join its Civil Rights Division, the part of the office handling discrimination laws. True to its philosophy, it stressed that it welcomed applications from those with "targeted disabilities." As well as deafness, blindness, and other physical impairments, the accepted disabilities included "mental retardation" and "mental illness."

A GOVERNMENT EMPLOYMENT OFFICE in Thetford, Norfolk, banned a recruitment company in 2010 from displaying a job advertisement for a cleaner that expressed a requirement that the successful candidate be "very reliable and hard working." The office told the company, headed by Nicole Mamo, that the ad could not be run in case unreliable people sued for discrimination.

THE NEW YORK TIMES, reporting in 1992 on a new regulation from the Department of Agriculture, reflected that while the Lord's Prayer contained 56 words, the 23rd Psalm 118 words, and the Ten Commandments 297 words, the department's just-released directive on the pricing of cabbage needed no fewer than 15,629.

AN AUDIT BY THE U.S. Department of Justice released in January 2008 revealed that a number of telephone tapping operations against criminal and terrorist groups run by the Federal Bureau of Investigation had collapsed because the FBI had failed to pay its bills and had been cut off by the telephone company. The review found that more than half of a thousand bills sampled had not been paid on time. At least one wiretap conducted under the Foreign Intelligence Surveillance Act, covering the most sensitive of the U.S. Government's espionage operations, had had to be abandoned because of "untimely payment." The report added: "We also found that late payments have resulted in telecommunications carriers actually disconnecting phone lines established to deliver surveillance results to the FBI, resulting in lost evidence." In one unidentified field office, the outstanding bill had reached $66,000.

THE CENTRAL COMMAND OF Russia's Strategic Rocket Force base at Odintsovo, near Moscow, had its electricity supply cut for an hour and a half in September 1995 because it had failed to pay its bills. Power was restored only when an emergency payment of $6.75 million was made.

A RUSSIAN GOVERNMENT AMNESTY of petty criminals in Moscow in 2000 was followed by a spate of thefts from private garages around the city. Dozens of cars were stolen without any apparent sign of break-in. Police were mystified until they delved into the national prison service's social reintegration program. Designed to train inmates in useful trades, prisons had taken on contracts to manufacture a range of products, one of which was padlocks. "It was pretty simple," a spokesperson said. They make the locks in jail and, when they come out, they open them."

THE AUSTRIAN JUSTICE MINISTRY introduced a money-making scheme for its prisons service in 2008 by setting up telephone call centers run by inmates on behalf of large consumer service providers. Controversy erupted when it emerged that most of the prisoners employed turned out to be inside for fraud or other financial crime, and that their tasks included extracting customers' personal details to be used for marketing purposes. Consumer organizations attacked the program, which had been set up against the opposition of prison administrators, for allowing information to get into the wrong hands. Customers were not aware they were speaking to convicted prisoners, who presented themselves as employees of the service provider, usually a telecoms company. Asked to explain the choice of prisoner recruited for the jobs, the Justice Ministry said that the scheme preferred convicted fraudsters because they were "experienced sales geniuses."

AN ELEVEN-MONTH-OLD CHICAGO BABY was granted a gun license by the state authorities when they responded to a prank application sent in by his father. Howard "Bubba" Ludwig, who had "signed" the form with a squiggle guided by his father, also named Howard, received the license despite the inclusion with the application of a genuine photograph of the baby and personal identification information recording that he was two feet three inches tall and weighed 20 pounds.

TOURIST JOE ADKIN, FROM Chesterfield, Derbyshire, picked up his wife's passport by mistake when going on vacation in March 2002. He got through check-in, passport control, and boarding at Gatwick Airport. He was only stopped, by the Spanish authorities, when he arrived at Lanzarote.

A FIRE CREW DISPATCHED from the Niles fire department in Ohio in January 2004 refused to put out a blaze destroying a man's house because they found it was 200 yards outside their city boundary. They waited until another crew from the neighboring Weathersfield fire department arrived just to ensure no one was injured. The distraught owner, Jason Radcliff, complained that his house could have been saved if the first crew had acted as soon as they arrived. The Niles crew were backed up by their superiors, who told press that the unit should never have been dispatched in the first place.

A SPELLING MISTAKE LED the Danish air force to unwittingly hire a haulage company from communist East Germany to help build secret hangars designed for NATO aircraft. It should have been Austrian. The mistake was not noticed until an East German articulated truck arrived at the Tirstrup air base in Jutland in November 1988. The driver produced papers proving his company had been contracted to transport material to the site. The slipup appeared to stem from the Danish words for Austria—Østrigsk—and East Germany—Østtysk—being so similar. "We thought we had got an Austrian firm to do the job, so we were somewhat shocked to find an East German truck on the site," said Lieutenant Colonel Egon Beck, the commander of the base.

THE AUSTRALIAN GOVERNMENT POLICE mission on peace-keeping duty in Cyprus shared its secrets with the Soviets for an unknown period in 1988 until the discovery that all its messages back home had been going to the Soviet mission in Canberra instead of the police HQ nearby. The telex numbers differed by one digit. The mistake was discovered when an officer arrived back claiming his leave had been approved. When the papers could not be found, the truth dawned. The Soviets had been responding to routine messages on leave and overtime in the hope of netting significant material later.

IN JANUARY 2010, THE Israeli Government laid on an exhibition of stolen ancient artifacts that had been recovered from criminals to educate the public about the problem of black marketeering in looted art. The display, in an Ashdod museum, was raided by thieves and several of the items were lost again.

MOVING IN MYSTERIOUS WAYS

The Greenville County Department of Social Services, South Carolina, sent notification to a resident who had died in 1992 terminating his financial support, as follows: "Your food stamps will be stopped effective March 1992 because we received notice that you passed away. May

God bless you. You may reapply if there is a change in your circumstances."

ACCORDING TO THE *BEELD* newspaper in 1993, a farmer who had applied to the South African Directorate of Financial Assistance in 1944 for a grant had just received a response—49 years later—asking him to provide more details—"as a matter of urgency." The farmer had been dead since 1964.

RAVINDRA HALDER, WHO APPLIED for a job in a state employment exchange office in Calcutta, received an invitation to attend an interview—34 years later, in March 2002. Now aged 52, and a grandfather, he was ruled out because of his age. "I'd given up hope. I'd applied in 1968. I'm now too old for a government job." Halder still held out hope for his son, who had put his name down for a post in the same office four years earlier but had not yet been called. Minister of Labor for West Bengal, Mohammad Amim, was quoted as acknowledging that it often took "a long time" for a person to be called for an interview.

SICILIAN GERLANDO PETRUCCI WAS offered a school caretaker's job 22 years after he had applied for it. By the time he received the notification inviting him to report ("immediately") to his new post in Brusasco in the north of Italy, Petrucci had accumulated a 20-year career as a customs officer, and had no desire to move to the other end of the country. He declined the offer.

THE INDIAN STATE OF Karnataka settled a 34-year dispute with one of its doctors in 2004, which produced a $48,000 payment to compensate the medic for not having made him work for nearly two decades. R. M. Sardesai, who had once worked in a primary health center in Bijapur district, had stayed at home in 1970 because, he claimed, he had not been notified of his next posting. He remained unoccupied for the next 19 years, later saying that it was the government's fault if he was not sent on duty. The case eventually came to light only because he lodged a claim for salary increases he would have been entitled to over the years had he been properly posted. A tribunal ruled that he was officially "on leave" for the first two years but "waiting for posting" for the next 17. The state could not explain why it had lost track of him in its posting system.

PARESH BARUAH, A TERRORIST who had waged a 30-year war against the Indian government in the state of Assam in the east of the country, was formally sacked in 2010 after the government discovered he was still on the books of the state-run railway company and had been receiving his pay as a porter even though he had not turned up for work since 1979.

THE ROMANIAN STATE TELEPHONE company replied to customer Gheorghe Titianu in August 2004, 28 years after he had applied for a phone connection. The joy was short lived for Titianu, living in the remote northern town of Suceava, who was informed that there was no phone line yet available.

FIRE ENGINES HEADING TOWARD a fire in the Massachusetts town of Westfield in June 1999 were held up by a state toll-booth operator who insisted on charging each before letting the emergency vehicles proceed.

As POLITICAL AND MILITARY analysts disputed Western intentions in the spring of 1999 on whether the United States would intervene in Kosovo, more astute observers were confident of the inevitability of war several weeks before the event. Three weeks before the invasion, an insignia-making factory in Texas openly announced that it had just received a rush order from the Pentagon…for 9,000 Purple Heart medals.

WITH 14 MONTHS TO go before the arrival of the year 2000, the Kenyan government set up in the autumn of 1998 a commission to investigate the potential threat of the millennium bug, the computer chip flaw that experts predicted would bring chaos to the world's electronics. The commission was given 18 months to deliver its report.

FROM THE HISTORY BOOKS

Although Latin America features strongly in any review of political upheavals, the next most persistently volatile system of government is, surprisingly, that of the French. The Third Republic, which ran for 70 years between 1870 and its demise in the Nazi invasion of 1940, enjoyed no fewer than 88 governments. On seven occasions (1877, 1913, 1917, 1930, 1932, 1933, and 1934) the country had four governments holding office within the year. At its most frenetic, France had nine different administrations in the 33 months between February 1932 and November 1934.

The Fourth Republic, which followed in 1946, was arguably more chaotic, albeit mercifully shorter lived. It was the time when being French prime minister became a byword for uncertainty. In its 12-year duration, it saw 21 separate governments. Only two ruled longer than a year. Three lasted for less than a month. It was eventually abolished by Charles de Gaulle in 1958, bringing to an end an inglorious period in French governance that had seen, if we include the Occupation and Provisional governments during the Second World War, a grand total of 115 administrations in 88 years, a rate—which, astonishingly, the people put up with for nearly a century—of a change of government every nine months.

HISTORIANS CAN'T QUITE AGREE on how many changes of government Bolivia has had since independence in 1825. Up until the restoration of civilian government in 1982, Bolivia suffered 193 (some say only 189) coups in 157 years, making it modern history's most systemically unstable country.

SEVENTEENTH-CENTURY POLAND PROBABLY HAS the dubious honor of creating history's worst method of parliamentary governance. Commencing in the early 1500s, Poland enjoyed its golden age as the second largest state in Europe, and the wealthiest in the east. The Polish nobility forcefully developed the authority of the national Parliament, the Sejm. The Polish crown was entirely in its thrall, having to convene it every two years, and being forbidden to dismiss any government official or raise an army without Parliament's approval. It became the most powerful example in Europe of a legislative body controlling royal authority, long before the rest of the continent's assemblies had even tried. The seeds of ruin were sown, however, in 1652 when the nobility bizarrely introduced a rule—intended to reflect the principle of legal equality among members—that every member of the Sejm had to agree to any measure for it to pass. A single voice objecting was sufficient to block business entirely, even to dissolve the assembly itself, which under Polish law also nullified all acts passed during the session. Not unexpectedly, the working of the Parliament became paralyzed, there were frequent dissolutions, and the veto powers were exploited by foreign influences, to the point when, just over a century later, Poland's three big neighbors—Russia, Prussia and Austria—moved in and partitioned it. Not until 1791 was the liberum veto abolished. And not until 1918 would Poland reemerge as a sovereign state again.

ARGENTINA HAD FIVE DIFFERENT presidents in 13 days during an economic crisis at the end of 2001. On December 21, Fernando de la Rúa, facing riots in the streets, resigned as president two years into his term of office. Constitutionally, Ramón Puerta, the Senate leader, became temporary president. Congress elected Adolfo Rodríguez Saá two days later, but he lasted for a week before resigning himself and leaving the office to Eduardo Camaño, the leader of the lower House of Congress (because the Senate had not replaced its leader), who took over on New Year's Eve. Eventually, on January 2, Congress found Eduardo Duhalde, a losing candidate in the last presidential election, willing to take on the poisoned chalice.

HAITI HAD SIX GOVERNMENTS in 1991 during a period of turbulence surrounding the election—and almost immediate overthrow by the army—of reformist civilian President Jean-Bertrand Aristide.

CHILE HAD SEVEN CHANGES of presidency between July and December 1829 during the country's short-lived civil war.

IN AN UNSTABLE PERIOD immediately following its declaration of independence in 1838, Honduras had nine different occupants of its presidency between January and September 1839.

EL SALVADOR HAD 53 governments in its first 50 years after becoming independent in 1821. This included 7 in the two and a half years between March 1832 and October 1834, 13 in the decade of the 1840s and 14 in the 1850s. To 2010, its 189-year history has seen 94 governments.

SHORTLY AFTER IT GAINED independence from France in 1946, Syria suffered 11 changes of prime minister between March 1949 and December 1951, an average of once every three months.

 MEXICO HOLDS THE DISTINCTION of having three presidents in a single day, and therefore the world's shortest-serving president. On February 18, 1913, a notorious day in the country's history, President Francisco Madero was overthrown by the army commander Victoriano Huerta. To give legal cover to his coup, Huerta allowed Foreign Minister Pedro Lascuráin, constitutionally next in line to be president, to take office and got him to install Huerta as his interior minister, which under the constitution was the next office in line for the presidency. Lascuráin resigned within the hour. Accounts vary as to exactly how long he was in office—either 15 or 55 minutes—but Mexico had its third president of the day by sunset.

POSTWAR ITALY, OFTEN THE example of instability that comes to the modern mind, has by these yardsticks a modest record for fluidity. It is on its 61st government in the 64 years since the foundation of the republic in 1946. Giulio Andreotti served as prime minister no fewer than seven times, all between 1972 and 1992. Giovanni Giolitti, who was premier five times between 1892 and 1921, was once asked whether governing Italy was difficult. "Not at all," he replied, "but it's useless."

THE RECORD FOR MOST prime ministerships appears to be Belgian leader Wilfried Martens, who headed eight separate governments in his country between April 1979 and December 1987.

FOR A FULLY FLEDGED parliamentary democracy, Britain's recent record for lengthy office holding is notable. The country had just three prime ministers in the 28 years between Margaret Thatcher taking office in 1979 and Tony Blair leaving office in 2007.

6

POWER AND THE GLORY: HIGH OFFICE

Leadership brings its own demands. Some are born great, some achieve greatness...well, we're not interested here in those who made a success of it. We're turning the spotlight on those leaders for whom the burden of being at the top of the tree proved rather more than they could cope with and whose travails, often in the glare of the public eye, demonstrate that fame can be the most poisonous of chalices. Others, though, seemed to embrace high office for all it could give...and, it seemed, then some more.

I AM THEIR LEADER...

To recognize his country's oil shortage, Ugandan leader Idi Amin turned up at Entebbe International Airport by bicycle in April 1976 for the arrival of the visiting president of neighboring Rwanda.

TANZANIAN PRESIDENT JULIUS NYERERE issued instructions to his ministers in 1979 to ride bicycles to work to conserve fuel. He said it would also reduce "the pot bellies carried around by some party and government leaders." It is not known whether any minister complied.

JAPANESE PRIME MINISTER TAKEO Fukuda served his cabinet with a luncheon of watermelon and peaches from an area of the country stricken with cholera in the summer of 1977 to calm public fears about contaminated food. He then left without touching his portion.

IT WAS CLEARLY A sensible option. When Peru suffered a similar cholera outbreak in 1991, fisheries minister Félix Canal Torres mounted his own televised stunt to reassure the public. He had his president, Albert Fujimori, and the country's agriculture minister join him in a meal of raw fish to prove it was safe for human consumption. Local press noted somewhat skeptically that the nation's health minister had declined the invitation. The next day, Torres fell ill—with cholera.

THE EUROPEAN UNION FOOD and farm commissioner, Franz Fischler, missed the launch of the European Food Safety

Authority in January 2002 due, it was believed, to his having been struck down with food poisoning. He was scheduled to preside over the inauguration of the authority, whose purpose was to provide an EU-wide early warning system for food safety scares.

ANTONIO NUNES, HEAD OF the Portuguese Food Standards Agency, which was in charge of policing the country's new ban on smoking in public places that came into force at the start of 2008, was caught in the early hours of New Year's Day lighting up a cigar in a casino on the outskirts of Lisbon. Although the official enforcer of the legislation, he claimed to journalists that he thought the rules did not apply to casinos. His government colleagues helpfully told him they certainly did.

Five months later, his own prime minister was embarrassingly caught having a cigarette on a Portuguese aircraft covered by the ban. José Sócrates was flying on an official trip to Venezuela in May and lit up once the first class curtain had been drawn across the cabin that shielded him from regular passengers. He was forced to apologize and promised to stem his habit. So far as is known, no formal action was taken against either politician.

THE DEFENSE MINISTER OF the West African state of Ivory Coast performed one of the oddest of state functions in April 2002 when he was called in by the national football association to lead a forgiveness ceremony with witch doctors after the team had reportedly reneged on paying for their services 10 years earlier. The country had won the 1992 African Championships, supposedly with the help of the witch doctors, but had never paid them after their success. There followed a decade of abysmal performances, and they had just failed to qualify for the 2002 World Cup. Summoning the heavy political guns, the national coach got Moisa Lida Kouassi to lead a meeting with the witch doctors to seek their forgiveness for the apparent curse. Presenting them with alcohol and an undisclosed amount of cash, he told the sorcerers, "I ask pardon for the unkept promises." The team successfully qualified for the next two World Cups (in 2006 and 2010) and since 2006 has been successively runners-up, fourth, and quarter-finalists in the African Championships.

GRAND SCHEMES

To mark more than three decades in power, Félix Houphouët-Boigny, president of the West African state of Ivory Coast, one of the world's poorest nations with a $10 billion debt, diverted over $300 million of his country's scarce finances to

building a near full-size replica of Rome's
St. Peter's Basilica in his remote home village
of Yamoussoukro. Air conditioned, and only

slightly smaller than the real St. Peter's after discreet Vatican
pressure, it was capable of holding 18,000 people inside, and a
further 300,000 in a colonnaded esplanade. Only 30,000
people then lived in Yamoussoukro. Taking four years to complete, it was inaugurated by Pope John Paul II in an elaborate ceremony in September 1989. The 80,000 square feet of
stained-glass windows were nearly three times that of
Chartres Cathedral. One window portrays Houphouët-Boigny
as one of the Magi, presenting a gift to Jesus.

JOAQUIN BALAGUER, DICTATORIAL PRESIDENT of the Dominican
Republic, the small and poverty-stricken Caribbean
nation claimed (only by the Dominicans) to be the first
landfall of Christopher Columbus when he arrived in the
New World, plowed an estimated $70 million into build-
ing a 688-foot-tall, 10-story monument in his capital
Santo Domingo for the 500th anniversary celebrations of
Columbus's arrival in 1992.

El Faron a Colón (the Columbus lighthouse) was both
a lighthouse—shaped as a reclining cross with 149 powerful lights capable of beaming the shape of a cross into the

night sky, and visible from Puerto Rico 150 miles away—
and a mausoleum to Columbus's supposed bones, even
though historians doubt that the island was in fact the first
landing place of the explorer.

The construction was almost as heroic an enterprise,
given that half the population lived below the poverty line
and the country regularly experienced eight-hour daily
power cuts. Most of the fish at the national aquarium had
died in 1990 because a power failure starved them of oxygen.
The project required 50,000 shanty homes to be demolished.

Balaguer had asked the Pope to officially inaugurate
it, as he had honored the Ivory Coast spectacle. This time,
John Paul diplomatically decided to arrive later in the week
for his Mass. Amid huge public outcry at the folly, only
100,000 people turned up for the blessing. The Pope's previous visits had attracted crowds of a million or more. The
light has rarely been switched on since. When it is, it drains
most of the supply from the rest of the neighborhood.

IN AN ECHO OF Balaguer's largesse, Abdoulaye Wade, the
83-year-old president of poverty-wracked Senegal in West
Africa, inaugurated his own monument to excess in April 2010
when he marked the 50th anniversary of the country's independence by spending $27 million on a massive 160-foot-tall

bronze statue celebrating "African Renaissance." It stood taller than the Statue of Liberty, and being built on a hill in the capital, Dakar, made it, in all, taller than the Eiffel Tower.

Depicting a three-figure combination of a man holding up a child, with a seminaked woman in tow, it sparked controversy in the deeply Muslim country, where the amount of flesh exposed was condemned by local religious leaders. Wade proudly claimed that the monument was designed to last a minimum of 1,200 years. Insiders told of the fraught architectural battles behind the construction. Senegal's original choice of builders, South Korea, concluded that the hill it is on would not support its weight. Wade turned to North Korea, who accepted the challenge. The elderly president, already entering his second decade as leader, and who had courted further controversy by announcing earlier in the year his intention to stand for reelection again in 2012, added fuel to the fire by declaring that he would take 35 percent of the revenue the statue would generate from tourists because the monument had been all his idea.

THE SELF-ESTEEM OF ANOTHER African leader got the better of him in 2009. President Denis Sassou-Nguesso, dictatorial strongman of Congo-Brazzaville, published a book of political thoughts with a foreword claimed to be from Nelson Mandela.

Except that Mandela denied all knowledge of having written anything for the notoriously autocratic despot. Under the ironic title "Straight Speaking for Africa," the foreword had Mandela praising the Congolese leader as "a man who is not only one of our great African leaders...but also one of those who...worked tirelessly to free oppressed peoples from their chains and help restore their dignity and hope." Mandela's foundation was last heard of contemplating legal action.

PHILIPPINE STRONGMAN FERDINAND MARCOS built a 99-foot-tall concrete bust of himself on the slopes of Mount Pugo in the north of the country at the height of his power in the early 1980s. It remained a landmark well after his removal from office in 1986 and his death in 1989. It was suddenly blown up in a nighttime raid in 2002, supposedly by treasure hunters who believed a long-held legend in the Philippines that Marcos had found, and stored in the giant head, a haul of treasure left behind by the occupying Japanese in the Second World War.

IRAQ'S SADDAM HUSSEIN TOOK delivery in September 2000 of a copy of the Koran that he had had written in his own blood. Iraqi media reported that it was the president's way of giving thanks to God for escaping unharmed (so far) in his long career. The 605-page book had taken three years to finish. It was later placed in the Mother of all Battles mosque in Baghdad, completed in 2001 to commemorate Saddam's 1990 invasion of Kuwait. The mosque, adorned with sayings of Saddam and a plaque of his signature 10 feet long, boasted eight minarets. Four were shaped like Kalashnikov rifle barrels and four resembled Scud missiles. Each was 43 meters tall, representing the "43 days of U.S. aggression" in 1991. A reflecting pool ringed the building in the shape of the Arab world. In the middle lay a monument of Saddam's thumbprint with his initials in gold.

THE PERSONALITY CULT THAT grew up around Chinese leader Mao Tse-tung may have held back the country's economic and military advance. According to the *Cuizhou Daily* in 1994, the 4.8 billion metal lapel badges that China produced during the Cultural Revolution, which became mandatory adornments for loyal citizens to wear, used up aluminum that could have made 39,600 MiG jet fighters.

(IN)DIGNITIES OF OFFICE

Bill Skate, prime minister of Papua New Guinea, arrived for an official visit to Indonesia in 1998 without his luggage. His national airline, Air Niugini, forgot to offload his baggage before leaving. It had, however, delivered his wife's. So the premier donned his spouse's attire, which was reported to include flowing, silky slacks, for the official welcoming ceremony, while his own clothes were hurriedly laundered locally. The episode only emerged when Skate was asked questions about the sudden, and otherwise unexplained, dismissal of the head of Air Niugini a few weeks later.

FOUR MONTHS AFTER ENTERING office, Bill Clinton caused a political storm in May 1993 by keeping the presidential entourage waiting for nearly an hour at Los Angeles International Airport while a celebrity Beverly Hills stylist gave him a haircut on board *Air Force One*. The appointment caused a 56-minute closure of two runways, leading to dozens of planes coming into land having to circle overhead. Clinton's press spokesperson fended off critics: "The president has to get his hair cut like everybody else and this was a convenient time to do it."

ITALY'S PRIME MINISTER SILVIO Berlusconi, whose electoral antics with showgirls have already been covered in chapter 2, showed no signs of retreating from his increasingly outlandish behavior when he celebrated the birthday of one of his woman MPs in January 2010.

He invited Michaela Biancofiore, who was not quite half his age, to mark her 39th birthday at his villa outside Milan. The cake depicted the MP with outsized breasts and the prime minister with his arms around her. Biancofiore denied anything improper happened at the event, and even claimed she had ordered the cake. Only the previous month, Berlusconi had come in for ridicule from the Italian press for reportedly whiling away time during a crucial international meeting on climate change in Brussels by drawing a series of doodles of thongs, stockings, and garters and passing them to his fellow leaders under the title "Women's Underwear through the Ages."

POLITICAL, AS MUCH AS physical, stature dominated the Sarkozy approach to image making. Critics lambasted the relaunch of the president's official website in March 2010, the day after he had finally dined with Barack Obama in a prolonged effort to restore Franco-American relations after their breakdown over Iraq. The new site appeared to be a "cut-and-paste" of the White House design, using almost identical layout, font style, and colors. Even the "stay connected" section at the end of the front page had been slavishly translated as "restez connecté." Designed to also lift the president domestically after catastrophic local elections earlier in the month, it added to his stuttering image when English users discovered the sound translation of Sarkozy's biography contained what one UK newspaper correspondent termed language "worthy of Inspector Clouseau," describing Sarkozy as the "president of ze franche république."

THE KING AND QUEEN of Sweden caused a diplomatic flap in April 2006 when returning from their Easter vacation in neighboring Norway. Carl XVI Gustaf and Silvia stopped at a gas station to refuel but drove off without paying. The "well-groomed couple" were only recognized when station attendants reran CCTV footage to identify the miscreants. The royal household later blamed their chauffeur.

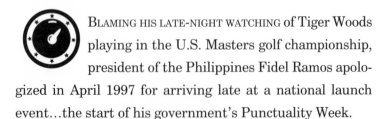 BLAMING HIS LATE-NIGHT WATCHING of Tiger Woods playing in the U.S. Masters golf championship, president of the Philippines Fidel Ramos apologized in April 1997 for arriving late at a national launch event...the start of his government's Punctuality Week.

IN THE PUBLIC EYE

German chancellor Gerhard Schroder was so stung by media stories that he dyed his hair that he went to court in April 2002 to have the allegations legally stopped. An image consultant had told the DDP news agency that he thought the chancellor should stop tinting gray streaks in his dark brown hair. Schroder, who faced a general election later in the year, took the claim with unexpected sensitivity, claiming that to accuse him of coloring his hair—which he denied—amounted to accusing him of being "an established liar." The case necessitated Udo Walz, Berlin's star hairdresser who barbered the 58-year-old chancellor, to submit a deposition to the court refuting the claim that the hair was dyed, "It is indeed unusual for a man his age not to have gray hair," he told the press, but said "a hairdresser could tell" if there was artificial coloring. However, a former wife emerged to claim, in contrast, how he would use a toothbrush to apply cream to his eyebrows before press interviews. The affair gripped the usually stolid German press for a month until, in May, the court ruled that the broadcaster had been wrong to air the claim without making an effort to verify it. Schroder's demand for a retraction was granted and DDP duly broadcast his denial. The case was thought to have cost thousands of euros of public money defending the chancellor. In September, Schroder retained power in a narrow win in the election.

PAKISTAN LEADER ASIF ZARDARI announced in July 2009 that he was banning political jokes that ridiculed his presidency. The country's Federal Investigation Agency had been instructed to investigate any quip sent by email or text message or posted on an Internet blog. Notoriously thin skinned about his reputation, Zardari announced he would use the newly introduced Cyber Crimes Act to outlaw "ill-motivated" comments about his leadership. The move came as the president's official email account was reportedly being deluged with jokes and sarcastic comments as his popularity (as husband of the assassinated Benazir Bhutto) waned.

STYLES OF LEADERSHIP

Newly crowned King Abdullah of Jordan carried on in the tradition of his father in 2000 when it was reported that he had slipped out of the royal palace one night in heavy disguise to observe how his people lived. He spent the night at a public hospital 20 miles outside the capital, Amman, to find out for himself the state of health care in his country. Having rarely been seen in public before his accession less than a year earlier, few of his compatriots recognized him (a problem that foiled his father by the end: having ruled for nearly 50 years, he was frequently recognized on his nightly visits). He returned to the palace to voice criticism of the quality of the service being provided.

ANALYSTS NOTED IN 2000 possible signs of political reform in Morocco, a traditionally austere and conservative country. According to seasoned observers, one indicator that a warmer attitude to social integration might be emerging was the change of practice of young King Mohammed VI, who had succeeded six months earlier: his motorcades were now reported to be stopping at red traffic lights.

ERNIE FLETCHER, GOVERNOR OF Kentucky, applauded a campaign to improve fitness in his state by signing into law a Wellness and Physical Activity Initiative in April 2006. Calling it a "vital measure" that would "bring greater focus on combating the lifestyle issues that are destroying the health of Kentuckians," Fletcher urged people to take up the opportunities afforded by the program for a healthier life. These did not, it seems, apply to himself. He insisted on retaining use of his limousine to ride from his official mansion to the governor's office—a distance of 500 feet. A local newspaper added, "There is not a river, swamp, or alligator between them."

THE MOST EXTREME RECENT example of a personality disorder taking over a country has been Saparmurat Niyazov, president of the former Soviet republic of Turkmenistan in Central Asia. First as the local Communist boss and then as leader of the newly independent country, Niyazov led his people for 21 years until his death in 2006. Glorying in his title of Turkmenbashi ("Father of all the Turkomans"), he engineered a semireligious style of leadership, was revered as a prophet, and had every significant facet of the nation named after him. Streets, schools, airports, cities, even yogurt and a perfume took on his name. A dahlia was named after him, and planted all around the capital, which led to the banning of most pets in the city in order not to overpower their fragrance. The president decreed that residents could own only one cat, one dog, or a decorative bird. His presence also reached beyond the borders of Turkmenistan. Officials named a star in the constellation of Taurus and a crater on the moon in his honor.

When he was not renaming places, he was recasting the very fabric of his people's lives. In 2002, he renamed the months of the year. January became Turkmenbashi after himself; he renamed other months after national poets and writers, and April after his mother. He also renamed the days of the week with inspirational titles: Monday he named after himself, Turkmenbashi Day; Tuesday became Young Day; Saturday, Spirituality Day. The president would regularly take to the nation's airwaves to read his latest poetry, and his 400-page book of philosophical writings— the *Ruhnama Book of the Soul*—became required reading in schools. Children had to memorize it, and copies on display at places of worship had to be kissed by visitors. Every office of government was required to spend an hour a week discussing it. Motorists had to attend a 16-hour course on it in order to pass the driving test and get a license. On his 63rd birthday in 2003, he was officially bestowed the title of prophet by his fawning ministers.

He turned his downbeat capital of Ashgabat into what one observer called "a temple of kitsch," with outlandishly large public monuments springing up, most lavishly topped off in gold. Dozens of statues of the president and his late and esteemed mother were strewn around. There were estimated to be 10,000 statues in the country by the time of his death. The most notorious folly was a $9.7 million, 250-foot-tall marble arch, topped with a gold statue of the president that rotated during the day so it always faced the sun. In 2003, he bizarrely had built the world's longest shoe as a symbol of the "great strides" Turkmenistan had made under his leadership since independence from the

Soviet Union. Using 100 feet of leather, it measured 20 feet long and 5 feet tall. Its laces were 30 feet long. Its maker proudly declared, "There are no limits to our gratitude to our leader for the unlimited opportunities" Niyazov had bestowed on the country. In 2004 there were reports that he had started the construction of an ice palace three miles outside the capital so his people could go ice skating in one of the hottest countries on Earth.

His eccentricities took on a morbid streak in 2003 when a plot to assassinate him was uncovered. Niyazov went on national television to announce the date of the trial of the 32 alleged conspirators, and helpfully also told viewers the sentences that would be handed down—20 would be jailed and 12 exiled to remote parts of the country. He closed all hospitals outside the capital, and doctors were only allowed to study his book of writings and the medical works of an ancient Persian hero. As a result, illness and mortality rates soared to some of the worst on the planet.

In 2004, he banned beards and car radios, following up on his earlier bans on ballet, opera, and circuses, which he regarded as contrary to national traditions. The next year, he banned the playing of recorded music on national holidays, on television, and at private weddings. This ban was intended to protect traditional musicians from the "negative influences" of performers who mimed to records, Niyazov said. In 2006, a decree issued just weeks before new teachers' pay scales were to be introduced required all teachers to write newspaper articles praising the virtues of the leadership. Those failing to get into print faced lower salaries under the new scheme. Reports spoke of chaotic scenes—and the paying of huge bribes—in local newspaper offices across the country as teachers scrambled to get their articles submitted. Pages and pages of laudatory articles appeared over the following weeks. Teachers were also now required to take exams to demonstrate their knowledge of the *Ruhnama* in order to keep their jobs.

He rubbed his former overlords' noses in it when Russian leader Vladimir Putin made his first visit. Niyazov reportedly stretched the official banquet past midnight—by insisting on 42 toasts during the evening—so that he could boast later that Putin's visit had lasted two days.

When he died in 2006, he was buried in a 180-foot-wide gold-domed mosque, adorned with scripts from the *Ruhnama* inlaid around the inside, and built at the cost of $80 million. Two years later, his successor abolished the Niyazov calendar, turned off the power on his revolving

statue in the center of Ashgabat, and ordered its disman-
tling and removal to an outer suburb.

CUBAN LEADER FIDEL CASTRO became famed—or notorious,
depending on one's political proclivities—for treating his
people to lengthy political speeches, always covered slavishly by the state-controlled broadcaster. The record was
set in his New Year speech for 1998, when he regaled the
nation for a full seven hours, transmitted in its entirety on
national television. It narrowly beat his seven-hour 1986
address to the National Party Congress. In 1960, he made
the (still) longest speech to the United Nations General
Assembly, lasting 4 hours and 29 minutes.

FIREBRAND PRESIDENT OF VENEZUELA, Hugo Chavez, took
over the reins of the voluble Latin American leader when
he instituted a Sunday television broadcast that saw him
speak to the nation every week, frequently for more than six
hours at a time. In September 2007, he managed an eight-
hour nonstop address, from 11 a.m. to 7 p.m. Knowing he
had beaten Castro's record, his parting words as he signed
off were: "The first time in history." To mark his decade
in power in 2009, he planned to excel even this with a
four-day marathon starting on a Thursday and ending on

Sunday. He managed two four-hour sessions on the first day and a lengthy slot the next, but the promised continuation into Saturday never materialized for unexplained "technical difficulties," which also caused the cancellation of the regular Sunday edition.

POLITICS IN ECUADOR WERE enlivened for six months between August 1996 and January 1997 after the bizarre election to the presidency of Abdalá Bucaram Ortiz, a self-styled prankster using the nickname *El Loco* ("the crazy one"). Swept to power on a program championing the poor, Bucaram became an overnight cult figure in the region, renowned for his publicity-seeking antics. He boosted his popularity by launching mass social schemes named after himself: Abdalact, providing subsidized milk to the poor in cartons emblazoned with his picture; Abdalagua, which did the same with drinking water; and Abdalafono, which brought telephone connections to poor areas. Soon after his election, the president achieved a probable world first by being the first head of state to appear on national television alongside a suite of cavorting showgirls to launch his pop CD, "A Madman in Love." Opposition parties demanded he be examined by a psychiatrist. He took to leaving cabinet meetings to dance in impromptu street events, and became mired in corruption allegations. Street protests erupted in January 1997 as his promised reforms failed to materialize, and in the first week of February he was thrown out of office by the National Congress on the grounds of mental incapacity, fleeing to Panama for sanctuary.

THE "FATHER OF TUNISIA," Habib Bourguiba, who served as president for 30 years after independence from France, left obituarists with rich fare when he died, officially aged 96 (his family claimed he was nearer 100) in 2000. His mental decline during the 1980s had given rise to a welter of tales of his idiosyncratic behavior and bizarre leadership style. He disciplined underperforming or uncooperative ministers by spitting in their face. He made state appointments that he promptly forgot, leading at one point to Tunisia having two ambassadors to the United Nations. In the space of four days in October 1987, he appointed three different people to lead his political party. He once announced on live television, during a nationwide address, that he had only one testicle. He was eased aside in a bloodless coup in 1987 and lived out the rest of his life in seclusion.

THE TEST OF OFFICE

William Clark, selected as second-in-command at the State Department in 1981, was one of the least auspicious appointments in Ronald Reagan's first administration, causing a storm in his confirmation hearings before the Senate Foreign Relations Committee for his ignorance of the issues for which he would be responsible. A judge by background and one of the closest friends of the president, Clark astonished his audience by his apparent lack of awareness of current affairs. He said he had "no opinion" on the spread of nuclear weapons (the world was in a distinctly chilly phase of the Cold War), could not name the leaders of South Africa or Zimbabwe, and, when pressed on his thin knowledge, he said he was confident he would learn as he went along. Asked to define the administration's foreign policy, he replied, "Peace through strength." Asked to be more specific, he responded, "It would be presumptuous of me to give priorities...I'm not prepared to assess that."

Appalled members of the committee were unable to stop the appointment. He was voted into the post only through the Republican majority. He lasted less than a year in the role, but exited upward—to become national security advisor for 18 months and then, in 1983, to become secretary of the interior.

THE GENERAL MANAGER OF the national mint in Chile was sacked in 2010 for allowing thousands of coins to be released that misspelled the name of the country. No one noticed that the 2008 issue of 50-peso coins had "Chiie" instead of "Chile" until late in 2009.

FROM THE HISTORY BOOKS

Félix Faure, president of France since 1895, died of a stroke in February 1899 while having sex with his 30-year-old mistress in his office in the Elysée Palace. Attila the Hun is also reputed to have died while having sex. He burst an artery while consummating his 12th marriage. At least one Pope—and possibly three others, but sources are not in agreement—have died in similarly compromising circumstances. A history of the Papacy records that in the case of John XII, who ruled from 955 to 964, "no Pope ever went to God in a more embarrassing position." He was caught having sex with his latest mistress by the woman's husband, who beat the Pope with a hammer. Three days later, he died.

IF WE KNOW ZHAO Zheng, China's first "sovereign emperor" who unified the country in the third century BC, best today because of the terracotta army he left to guard his tomb in Xian, he had an even more bizarre way of making an impression on his people when alive. After managing to eliminate or annex the seven rival states into which China was then divided and proclaim, in 221 BC, unification, he decided he wanted to emphasize how his dynasty was the starting point for China. In 213 BC, he ordered all books that were not concerned with agriculture, medicine, or prognostication (he was an avid adherent of fortune-tellers) to be burned, thus creating a clean slate for history to begin again. Only the collection in the imperial library was spared. He also had 160 academics decapitated for good measure. He had little chance to recraft history himself. He died three years later, and within another four years the dynasty itself had collapsed into feudal infighting.

AFTER INHERITING THE MANTLE of the Russian crown from his mother, Catherine the Great, in 1796, Czar Paul I exhibited bizarre ways of maintaining the security of the royal court. At a time of great uncertainty in Europe, with the French Revolution inspiring rebellion to authority all over the continent, Paul instituted a manic program of self-protection. Any symbol of non-Russian influence was suspect. In 1797 he issued an edict imposing a rigid dress code for citizens, banning any styles that were associated with Western

Europe. The authorities enforced it vigorously, with people being stripped of offending articles in the street. Personal security concerns required that any occupant of a carriage had to stop and get out to be in full view of the royal police when the czar's entourage passed. Not surprisingly, the restrictions irked a society that had, under Catherine, flourished as a modernizing country. Paul was strangled in a palace coup in March 1801, little over four years after he had taken the throne.

KIM IL-SUNG, THE FOUNDER of the reclusive North Korean Communist dynasty, had every road in the country built with an extra lane for his own exclusive use. To mark his 65th birthday in April 1977, he was reported to have bought 40,000 gold Swiss watches bearing portraits of him and his son, Kim Jong-il, for distribution to loyal party members. For his 70th birthday, the regime unveiled the "Iuche Tower," named after Kim's code of official thinking. It was built with precisely 25,550 blocks of granite, one for each day of Kim's life.

TURKISH SULTAN ABDUL AZIZ reigned for just 15 years from 1861 until deposed and assassinated in a coup in April 1876, but in his short time in office his eccentricities and taste for largesse ruined the economy of the emerging Turkish state. He amassed an entourage of over 5,000 personal servants, including 400 musicians and 400 grooms. Among them was one man whose sole role in the household was to replace the royal backgammon board after use. Another was responsible for the task of cutting the royal fingernails, having no other function in between. He bought a collection of steam locomotives despite the fact that Turkey had no railway system—he developed the country's first network—and a fleet of modern iron ships, even though he did not have a navy that knew how to crew them. He mounted war games in his palace grounds for entertainment, using real soldiers from his army and live ammunition. For much of his reign, his annual personal expenditure ran at around £2 million, about $3.2 million. By the time he was ousted, Turkey had unsurprisingly slumped to a parlous state. Its overall debt amounted to £200 million (about $323,610,000), costing over £12 million annually ($19,416,600)—and half the national budget— just to meet interest payments. It would be the tipping point of the terminal decline of the Ottoman Empire.

HIS NEXT-BUT-ONE SUCCESSOR (ABDUL'S nephew Murad immediately followed but reigned for just 93 days before being deposed for insanity) took the burdens of high office equally bizarrely. Abdul Hamid II was a paranoiac par excellence. He built his own refuge palace at Yildiz a mile inland from the normal residences, which were all waterside locations next to the Bosporus, because he feared a waterborne attack. Yildiz was a surreal world in which the sultan closeted himself away for 30 years, with his existence constantly constrained by fear of being murdered. Literally hundreds of loaded guns were placed around the palace for Abdul's ready use. Some rooms were booby-trapped, with firearms released from hidden panels at the flick of a switch. The palace was designed by a 12-strong team of architects, but none knew of each other's existence, so that no one had a complete knowledge of the layout of the building. Rooms were deliberately cluttered with furniture designed to ensure that visitors entering could only arrive in single file. Most were entirely mirrored so that Abdul could see every angle. All had secret passages enabling a quick getaway. Abdul had any food tasted twice before accepting it, had his clothes "warmed" by an aide in case they had been laced with poison, and even had his documents baked and disinfected before being presented to him. He always wore chain mail under his clothes and a steel-lined fez. Even more bizarrely, certain language was barred in his presence or in papers to reduce the royal nervousness. "Revolutionary," "republic," and "freedom" were all forbidden. A chef who produced a menu with *bombe glacée* was reputedly sacked on the spot. Notoriously, when the king and queen of Serbia were assassinated in 1903 and their disemboweled bodies thrown out of a second-floor window, the Turkish press creatively reported that they had died of indigestion. Abdul endured his self-imposed isolation for decades, sending lookalikes to perform public functions in the city. He was eventually quietly deposed in 1909, and—after a lifetime of anxiety about a brutal death—died peacefully in his bed in 1918.

A TALE TO SHOW that however esteemed the leader or his office, human nature and fate can combine to reduce the aura of authority to some commonly recognizable basics. U.S. Army leaders at Fort Bragg, North Carolina, laid on an elaborate dupe operation in February 1968 when President Lyndon Johnson made a sudden visit to their base at the height of the Vietnam War and declared he wanted to meet a troop of the 82nd Airborne Division just as they were about to embark for the war zone. Given about nine hours' notice, the commanders found the request problematic, as the Vietnam-bound 3rd Brigade were by then fully engaged in an "all-day beer bust and barbecue" and would be in no condition to parade before the president. So the deputy commander ingeniously borrowed a battalion from one of the division's other brigades, which had only just returned from Vietnam, dressed them in battle fatigue without insignia and stood them in front of the 3rd Brigade's colors.

The plan had been for a straightforward inspection and presidential departure. According to the account that made the affair public nearly a decade later, as he walked down the ranks, the president shook hands with each of them, glowing fulsomely with praise: "God bless you, son...I'm proud of you, damned proud of you. I know you will serve the cause of freedom as your forefathers served it." The men, unaware of the ruse, began to mutter with concern "We're all going...We're going back to 'Nam." Johnson was not apparently aware of the bewilderment growing on the faces of the soldiers.

Aiming to bring the episode to a conclusion, base commander Major General Seitz sought to steer the president back to his car, diplomatically apologizing for "putting you way behind schedule." To Seitz's horror, Johnson, overcome by emotion, declared, "Schedule, Hell, forget the goddamned schedule, I came here to see those boys off, and I'm going to see them off." Seitz's team had to continue the charade by marching the increasingly anxious stand-in troops off to an air transport plane, load them on board under the watchful and tear-stained eye of the president, and start the engines. The plane carried on through the motions of taking off, with Johnson standing to attention, hand over heart, paying tribute to his "damned fine boys."

As soon as Johnson left, the plane landed and the relieved troops disembarked. The president never knew of the deception. In his memoirs, he recorded the visit as one of the most memorable of his term of office, adding, "It tore my heart out to send back to combat a man whose first son had just been born."

STANLEY BALDWIN, UK PRIME minister three times (1923–24, 1924–29, and 1935–37), told an acquaintance in 1935 how during his previous premiership he had worn his old school tie while traveling in a train. A man opposite noticed and asked, "You're Baldwin, aren't you? You were at Harrow in my time in '84." Upon Baldwin's acknowledgement, a lengthy pause followed, and then the man asked, "Tell me, what are you doing now?"

7

DARNED FOREIGNERS: DIPLOMACY

However much they are masters in their own back-yard, all politicians eventually have to accept they need to deal with their opposite numbers in countries large and small. How they do it can often mean the difference between war and peace. Testing one's own demands against those of others is fraught with potential for dispute. Diplomacy has been described as the art of putting your foot down without stepping on anyone's toes. Here we survey the recent international scene.

THE UNIQUE WORLD OF DIPLOMACY

Officials in the Italian Foreign Ministry staged a novel industrial demonstration in 1981 when a national strike of civil servants took place during a pay dispute. They undertook a "strike in reverse" and carried on working after the end of normal working hours. They refused to take meal breaks and continued their duties until 2 a.m. Union representatives said they had decided against a traditional walk-out because "professional habits" would lead most of the ministry staff to turn up anyway. But they did not want to undermine their colleagues' strike elsewhere in the service.

THE MAYOR OF ROME headed a delegation to Tunis in 1985 to sign a treaty formally restoring peace with the city of Carthage, which the ancient Romans had destroyed in 146 BC.

THE DUTCH AMBASSADOR IN Britain paid a long-overdue visit to the Scilly Isles off Cornwall in 1986 to sign a peace treaty between the Netherlands and the islands that brought to an end a state of war that had formally existed for 335 years. When Britain had settled its scores with the Dutch after war in 1651, no one had noticed that the Scillies had been left out. It was only in October 1985 that the chair of the isles' council discovered the oversight.

FRANCE AND SPAIN REACHED an agreement in 1986 to exchange about an acre of territory each on their joint border because a statue of Luis Companys, the last Republican president of Spain before the Franco revolt, had been built by mistake on French soil.

IN 1992, AFTER 18 years of legal wrangling, diplomats for India and Bangladesh agreed a 999-year lease on the Tin Bigha corridor, which links mainland Bangladesh with two enclaves in India, Dahagram and Angarpota. The size of the territory involved was the equivalent of a football field.

NEW MOORE ISLAND, A sandbar in the Bay of Bengal, was also the subject of protracted dispute between India and Bangladesh. For nearly 40 years, the two countries failed to settle ownership of the uninhabited island of 100,000 square feet—slightly smaller than London's Trafalgar Square—after it had emerged from the sea in the wake of the 1970 cyclone that devastated the region. The problem solved itself in March 2010 when an oceanographer at Jadavpur University in Calcutta announced that global warming and rising sea levels had caused the entire landmass to disappear back under the sea.

A GERMAN WATCHDOG OF government waste revealed in 1992 that the authorities did not even know where Germany's borders were. It discovered that 100,000 marks ($68,200) had been spent on a small bridge across the river Blies in the Saarland to access land officials believed was German. It later turned out that the land was actually part of France.

THE HEAD OF THAILAND'S Office of the Prime Minister, Somsak Thepsuthin, announced in December 2001 plans for a 27-hole golf course at the juncture of his country with Laos and Cambodia, with nine holes in each country, the first in the world to straddle three countries. Despite the possible downside of the area being littered with Khmer Rouge land mines from the wars of the 1970s, he was confident that golfers would fly in from around the world "for the challenge." To our knowledge, a decade later the course is still on the drawing board.

DISPUTED LOYALTIES

In 1982 the mayor of Key West and his council, frustrated by travel restrictions caused by U.S. Border Patrol roadblocks set up to stem the flow of illegal Cuban refugees that had severely damaged the tourist trade, declared secession from the United States and the establishment of the Conch Republic. Declaring, "We were once the richest town south of Savannah; now we're just the highest taxed," Dennis

Wardlow formally announced separation on April 23 in an elaborate ceremony in front of the roadblock at the entrance to the island chain, during which he was proclaimed prime minister and promptly declared war against America by ceremonially breaking a stale Cuban loaf over the head of an actor dressed in naval uniform. He rescinded the state of war after one minute and formally applied for $1 billion in aid from the United States.

The "republic" continues to this day, holding a celebratory week of events each year in April around "independence day" on April 23. The international airport at Key West is emblazoned with a banner welcoming arrivals to the Conch Republic, and sales of souvenir passports, ID cards, and car bumper stickers have become a staple ingredient of the once ailing tourist trade.

A GROUP REPRESENTING RESIDENTS of the District of Columbia, the federal territory that is home to the U.S. capital, Washington, marked American Independence Day in 2002 by seeking reaccession to the United Kingdom in protest of the lack of representation in the U.S. Congress, which sits on their doorstep. Despite years of lobbying, the other states, who need to approve the required constitutional amendment, have never summoned enough support to the cause. In 2000, the city authorities—elected local government has only existed since 1975—formally adopted as its official motto for car license plates the slogan "Taxation without representation." The protest group DC Vote presented a request to the British Embassy for the queen to reassume sovereignty over the city. Paul Strauss, the movement's leader, said, "We want Her Majesty to intercede on our behalf." There were no immediate signs that the British government was inclined to oblige.

TESTING RELATIONS

Muslim Pakistan refused permission for a delegation from the European Community to visit in 1982 because the team was headed by a man named Israel.

SOON AFTER TAKING OFFICE, U.S. president Barack Obama visited one of his arch opponents in the Americas in April 2009, Venezuela's firebrand leader Hugo Chavez. Obama graciously spoke at a news conference of the gift that Chavez had given him: "Well, I think it was a nice gesture to give me a book. I'm a reader." He had received Chavez's polemical study, *Open Veins of Latin America: Five Centuries of the Pillage of a Continent.*

IN NOVEMBER 2003, NEW Zealand prime minister Helen Clark was required by an airport guard to be frisked as a security risk as she went through metal detectors when changing planes in Sydney, Australia. Reports of the incident outraged New Zealand opinion, which regarded it as an insult by their traditional arch rivals. The guard was said not to have recognized the prime minister, despite her traveling with a sizeable official entourage.

GERMAN DEFENSE MINISTER VOLKER Rühe ruffled feathers during a period of controversy in the summer of 1992 as the country faced growing demands from its European allies to contribute troops to the NATO peace-keeping effort in the civil wars in the Balkans involving Serbia, Croatia, and Bosnia-Herzegovina. "I am not willing to risk the lives of German soldiers for countries whose names we cannot even spell properly."

NEGOTIATING AN AGREEMENT IN 1986 on sharing state-of-the-art military and industrial technology, the United States was acutely concerned about the ability of West Germany to keep such secrets safe from being leaked to the Communist East. How do we know? Details of the negotiation and the secret treaty were leaked to the West German newspaper.

THE FORMAL WELCOMING CEREMONY for the new West German ambassador to Honduras in 1989 was marred by a small but important oversight. The Honduran national military band had been unable to get the music for the German national anthem. They played the British one instead.

PROTOCOL SLIPUPS ARE LESS uncommon than might be thought. In November 2009, Venezuela's Hugo Chavez entertained his equally erratic counterpart from Iran when President Mahmoud Ahmadinejad visited. Unfortunately, he was welcomed by the playing of Iran's old imperial national anthem of the previous, overthrown, Shah's regime.

In October 1992, the U.S. Marine Corps caused a diplomatic storm with its northern neighbor by flying the distinctive Canadian maple leaf flag upside down during the national anthems ceremony at the opening game of the baseball World Series between Atlanta and Toronto. As images of the debacle at one of the biggest sporting events in North America were beamed across the continent, President Bush had to be roped in to issue a formal apology to his Canadian counterpart.

The White House did not help President Bush's visit to Southeast Asia in November 2006 by displaying on the president's official website the flags of the countries he was visiting. Included on the itinerary was Bush's first visit to Vietnam, always a sensitive affair for any American leader. The flag shown by the White House was the yellow and red emblem of the former U.S.-backed South Vietnam, a country that had been extinguished more than 30 years earlier by America's withdrawal.

When Bush visited Bulgaria in June 2007, every other American flag flying on poles spread along the ceremonial route down the main boulevard in the capital Sofia was the wrong way round—flying the starred blue quadrant on the right-hand side.

Australian officials caused a diplomatic incident with Spain in November 2003 at the opening ceremony in Melbourne of the two countries' match in the final of tennis' prestigious Davis Cup. Instead of playing the modern Spanish anthem, the tune that blared out across the stadium was the Communist Republican anthem used briefly in the 1930s during the Spanish Civil War. A version of the anthem includes a verse in which the Spanish Queen is beheaded and a man wipes his bottom on King Alfonso XIII, the grandfather of the present Spanish king, Juan Carlos. Unfortunately, the Spanish sports minister was present. He stormed out and the match only carried on after Australian diplomats had concocted a groveling apology for the slight.

It was not the first time Australia had slipped up. At a football World Cup qualifier match, also in Melbourne, with Israel in October 1985, the Australian hosts played, of all tunes, the West German national anthem for the Israelis.

OFFICIAL VISITS

Yoshiro Mori, who unexpectedly became Japanese prime minister in April 2000 after his predecessor suffered an incapacitating stroke, had a term of office that was both short—he lasted just a year and three weeks—and gaffe laden. A poor speaker of English, his advisors gave him emergency lessons before he departed on a crucial visit in May to see President Clinton in Washington. According to accounts that have become legendary in diplomatic circles, he was taught that when shaking hands with Clinton he was to say, "How are you?" Clinton would say, "I am fine, and you?" and Mori was advised, "Now you should say, 'Me too.' After that, the translators will do all the work for you."

On the big day, when greeting Clinton, Mori mistakenly asked, "Who are you?" Clinton, only slightly taken aback, responded jocularly, "Well, I am Hillary's husband, ha ha..." Mori replied confidently, "Me too, ha ha ha..."

UK RELATIONS WITH THE Gulf state of Qatar came within minutes of being derailed in the autumn of 1999 when British Department of Trade officials discovered an awkward inclusion in the dozen copies of a gift book that ministers were about to hand over to their Arab guests. Opting for a chic photography collection, *Britain: The Book of the Millennium*, they had neglected to notice one shot showing a model posing naked for art students. Civil servants were reported to have "felt-tipped away like mad" to cover up the picture in all 12 copies. Told of the episode, the author of the book acknowledged their problem: "There are no two ways about it—she's completely nude," adding, "I only hope they did it tastefully."

BRITAIN WAS ON THE receiving end of less than meticulous planning in March 2009 when Prime Minister Gordon Brown made his inaugural visit to the White House to meet newly elected president, Barack Obama. Aiming to shore up the "special relationship," Brown went armed with a gift of a first edition of the multi-volume biography of Winston Churchill. Obama reciprocated with a DVD box set of 25 famous Hollywood movies. When the British party returned home and tried to play them, they discovered they were Region 1 format, playable only in North America.

IT WASN'T THE ADMINISTRATION'S only blunder in its early days. Just three days after Brown's visit, Hillary Clinton, the new secretary of state, met her Russian counterpart Sergei Lavrov in Geneva. She gave him a joke gift of a small box the size of a television remote control with a single button on it. It was labeled, in Russian, a "reset" button, and was meant to be symbolic of President Obama's hope to recast U.S.–Russian relations after a stormy period under the previous Bush regime. Unfortunately, linguistic expertise seemed to have been in short supply, as a confused Lavrov quickly pointed out that the Americans had misspelled "reset." The word on the box translated as "overload." At least smiling, Lavrov told Clinton, who had spotted his quizzical expression when unwrapping the gift, "You got it wrong."

HILLARY CLINTON'S MONTH DID not get any better. On a visit to Mexico in late March, she visited the Basilica of Our Lady in Guadalupe, the second most visited Catholic shrine in the world and home to Latin America's equivalent of the Turin Shroud—a sixteenth-century cloak with an image of the Virgin Mary. The image is said to have miraculously appeared, and the phenomenon is unexplained to this day. Its local fame had clearly not extended to Clinton. Her first question to her host was, "Who painted it?" Rector Diego Monroy swiftly responded, "God!"

VISITING ISRAEL'S SACRED HOLOCAUST Museum in October 2000, German chancellor Gerhard Schroder performed a ceremony alongside the Israeli prime minister that should have involved him turning up the Eternal Flame memorializing those killed in the extermination camps. Instead, he turned the switch the wrong way and extinguished the flame. Horrified officials were initially unable to reignite the flame, which had been burning since 1961. It was eventually relit with a cigarette lighter.

BRAZILIAN PRESIDENT LUIS INACIO Lula da Silva made few friends on his visit to Namibia in November 2003 when he tried to compliment his hosts on his departure from the capital, Windhoek, saying it was so clean, it did not seem like Africa. "I'm surprised because…it doesn't seem like you're in an African country. Few cities of the world are so clean and beautiful as Windhoek." So far as we know, he has not been asked back.

THE BODYGUARDS OF AMERICAN secretary of defense William Perry were given a nasty surprise in January 1995 when he visited Pakistani tribesmen in the lawless hills near the Khyber Pass. As part of the reception ceremony, gun-toting elders danced in welcome, firing their automatic weapons in time to the music.

ALBANIA'S PUBLIC ORDER MINISTER had his official limousine confiscated by Greek customs when he arrived at the Christalopigi border crossing in December 1999 en route to an engagement in Athens. Spartak Poci's luxury Mercedes was subjected to a routine check that revealed the car to have been stolen in Italy. Embarrassed Greek officials said they had no option but to seize the vehicle, as Interpol had put out an order for its impounding. Stranded until his host sent up a Greek government car, Poci continued his journey to the Greek capital…to sign an agreement combating cross-border crime. He returned home by air.

AN OFFICIAL VISIT TO Washington in February 1996 by pomp-conscious French president Jacques Chirac—the first by a French leader for 12 years—nearly derailed when congressional leaders intimated to Gallic planners that they were unenthusiastic about granting him a joint session of Congress, the privilege usually accorded to America's closest allies. At the time, France was very unpopular in the United States on account of its controversial nuclear testing program in the Pacific. Chirac's threat to cancel the whole visit resulted in an elaborate subterfuge. According to diplomatic sources, while television cameras—and Chirac—witnessed a full chamber to listen to his speech, only 50 of the 535 seats were actually filled with congressional representatives. The rest were ushers and pages dragooned in to spare the president the humiliation of having no audience.

THE U.S. SECRET SERVICE mistakenly bombarded an Auckland chicken processing plant with top secret security details of President Clinton's arrival plans for the September 1999 Asia-Pacific Summit. Despite reporting the errant faxes, the head of the plant told local press that the messages kept arriving for several weeks. One detailed the installation of the White House secure communications equipment at Auckland airport ahead of the arrival of Air Force One, the president's plane. Another had the names of military officers involved in the advance party, replete with code names and security badge numbers. U.S. officials were reported to be "looking into the situation."

ANGER MANAGEMENT

For over three years, after a fit of pique about France's opposition to the U.S. war in Iraq, Walter Jones and Bob Ney, Republican members of the House of Representatives, persuaded the House cafeteria to rename French fries "Freedom Fries" and French toast "Freedom Toast" to express "our strong displeasure at our so-called ally, France." The practice was lifted in August 2006 as relations warmed. There was a touch of irony about the announcement: Jones had now become an outspoken critic of the war, leading him to express regret at starting the name-change campaign.

A LONG-AWAITED PEACE GATHERING between two tribes in the remote New Guinea highlands convened in 1990 with the intention of having a joint feast. Members of the Puman and Mandak tribes sacrificed a pig and proceeded to cook it. An argument broke out about the best way to prepare it, resulting in a five-day battle involving 2,000 spear-wielding warriors. Five died and dozens were wounded. A subsequent peace gathering agreed to have the event catered.

FOUR DAYS BEFORE THE end of the Bush administration in January 2009, the United States announced the imposition of increases to customs duties on a wide range of goods from the European Union. Commentators pointed to the possibility that Bush was still smarting from the lack of co-operation from France in the Iraq War, and the new tariffs contained a parting shot. While the duties on almost all the items were 100 percent, standing out was a 300 percent tariff on France's iconic product, Roquefort cheese. When quizzed, no one in the administration was willing to explain the reason for the decision.

Credence was lent to the move having had political motivation when the new Obama administration diplomatically negotiated a dropping of the tax four months later.

THE NADIR OF THE SUMMIT

The United Nations' flagship conference on international development in Monterrey, Mexico, in 2002 was marred by technical difficulties over sound and translation equipment because the UN had not checked that its contractors knew the right place to go. The German firm flew its technicians to Monterey, California, 1,500 miles away. It was halfway through the weeklong conference before they reached the correct destination.

ATTENDING THE 1989 CONFERENCE of the heads of state of the economic community of West Africa in Ouagadougou, Burkina Faso, Gambian president Dawda Jawara arrived in what the official British observer termed "an ostentatiously modest" propeller-driven aircraft. It was believed locally that this was designed to present an implicit contrast to the luxurious presidential jet enjoyed by the conference host, Blaise Campaoré. The slight managed to achieve more than intended. The propellers, which were still turning as the plane halted, sucked up the red carpet, chopping it to pieces and showering President Campaoré and other dignitaries with red fluff. It was then discovered, in the words of the British envoy's report, that the airport "proved not to possess steps of the right height to allow the Gambian president to descend gracefully to earth."

A BIZARRE DIPLOMATIC BALLET took place in the preparatory negotiations for the 1975 Conference on Security and Co-operation in Europe, a major milestone in managing Cold War relations between East and West. On the tricky question of who should fund the event, countries disagreed on whether the costs should be borne by the United Nations or by contributions by individual states. Tiny Luxembourg had not been able to afford to send a delegation to the talks and asked the Netherlands to represent its views. At the appropriate moment in the debate, the Dutch representative moved a few places across the conference hall to occupy the vacant Luxembourg seat and deliver a passionately argued statement demanding that the United Nations pick up the bill. Finishing the speech, he then moved back to his own seat and forcefully attacked the Luxembourg position, urging that all members should provide their own contributions.

FROM THE HISTORY BOOKS

In 1040, Pope Benedict IX initiated a vain attempt to make war illegal by proclaiming the "Truce of God," probably the first example of international attempts to outlaw war. It decreed that fighting was unlawful for anyone between vespers on Wednesday evening and sunrise on Monday.

THE SO-CALLED WAR OF 1812 between Britain and the fledgling United States is probably history's most extreme example of war by accident. It both began and ended through error. The conflict originated in American objections to British trade blockades that were thought to be trying to squeeze the life out of the new republic. The States eventually declared war on June 18, 1812. Unknown to them, over in England, a new government under Lord Liverpool had taken office 10 days earlier. Liverpool was in favor of a more conciliatory approach to America. He had had one of the key reasons for the war removed by withdrawing controversial orders allowing the conscription of American nationals into the British Navy. These orders had been rescinded just the day before the American declaration of war. The Americans could not have been aware of this, as there was no way for the news to reach Congress before it voted for war. Three more weeks, and news of the British climbdown would have been known. The war would last two and a half years and cost nearly 4,000 lives.

Its end was similarly shrouded in disastrous blunder. The culminating engagement, the Battle of New Orleans in early January 1815, took place two weeks after the official peace treaty ending the war had been signed on Christmas Eve 1814. News was still on its way from Europe and too late to prevent the final encounter. Nearly a thousand men lost their lives in the most unnecessary battle in history.

THERE ARE UNLIKELY TO be many competitors better suited for the title of Britain's most embarrassing diplomat of all time than Edward Hyde, Viscount Cornbury, who was appointed by his cousin Queen Anne in 1701 as governor-general of the New York colony. In an era steeped in the formalisms of courtly rectitude, he adopted the bizarre practice of donning women's clothes for public appearances. He turned up for his inaugural opening of the New York Assembly in 1702 dressed in a blue silk gown, a stylish diamond-studded headdress, and satin shoes. When challenged on the proprieties of his choice of clothes, he replied, "In this place and particularly in this occasion I represent a woman and ought in all respects to represent her as faithfully as I can." Described by contemporaries as a "large, fleshy man" with a distinctly masculine face, he preferred promenading around his domain in hooped skirts, flashing a womanly fan to waft away the city odors. Amazingly, despite the outrage his transvestism caused, he was not recalled until 1708.

RATHER MORE DIPLOMACY WAS shown by New York's city elders in June 1775 in the early months of the War of Independence when they faced the prospect of having to welcome both the newly appointed commander in chief of the rebel Continental Army, George Washington, and the return from England of the British governor of New York colony, William Tryon. They both arrived in the city on June 25. With only one main street—Broadway—available as a route for the ceremonial marching of the troops, the civic leaders laid on a welcoming reception for Washington and his force at the northern end of the thoroughfare, and for Tryon at the southern, downtown, end, ensuring that neither side managed to meet each other.

LABOR FOREIGN SECRETARY ERNEST Bevin, a trade union official to the core, had a typically working-class approach to the pomposities of diplomacy. Surprisingly appointed by Attlee in 1945 at a critical time of postwar reconstruction, his lack of finesse was sometimes an asset for the Foreign Office. Warned that he had to receive a puffed-up Guatemala ambassador who was arriving at the Foreign Office to stake a claim on the British Central American possession of Belize, Bevin warmly embraced the emissary when he was shown in with the greeting: "Guatemalia— that's where you're from, isn't it, Guatemalia...funny thing, we were just talking about it this morning, couldn't find it on the map. What a bit of luck you're here, now you can tell us where it is."

NINETEENTH-CENTURY GERMAN CHANCELLOR BISMARCK had an equally effective but more standard diplomatic device for retaining control. The story is told of the British ambassador who asked him during an audience how he handled "insistent visitors who take up so much of your time." Bismarck replied that "I have an infallible method. My servant appears and informs me that my wife has something urgent to tell me." At that point, there was a knock at the door and a servant entered bearing a message from his wife.

IN MARCH 1966, DURING the Cold War, the United States banned the importation of wigs that contained hair from people living in Communist countries.

JOHN HUMES, AMERICAN AMBASSADOR to Austria during the same era of confrontation, finding himself facing a similar quandary, applied a more freethinking approach. He had received a gift of a box of Cuban cigars at a time when dealing in any produce of the Communist regime would be a breach of U.S. sanctions policy. He therefore told his chief of staff to dispose of them with the following instructions: "Burn them…one by one…slowly."

8

LIFE IN THE UNDERGROWTH: LOCAL GOVERNMENT

They may be a million miles from the corridors of power, and far from the glare of the national media, but those engaged in the world of local politics are no less dedicated to the wielding of what limited authority they possess. At the lower levels of the political game, a paradox frequently prevails—that the smaller the issue, the more intensely the matter is pursued. Nowhere demonstrates better the human ability to turn the blandest of subjects into a political controversy, or the capacity to come up with the most novel of solutions. The concept of pettiness, in both senses, shines through. We see the small concerns of ordinary people getting dealt with, but often with the amazingly obsessive concern for formalism embodied by the tyranny of the petty bureaucrat. Somewhere, at some time, almost every problem

known to humanity has passed through the hands
of a local politician. Few have reached national
attention—until now. They deserve their rightful
place in the pantheon of political folly.

LOCAL ISSUES, LOCAL APPROACHES

In November 1983, the Planning Committee of the city council in Chico, California, voted 6–1 to make it a misdemeanour to drop a nuclear weapon inside the city precincts, punishable by up to a year in the county jail and a fine of $1,000. The community of 28,000, lying 150 miles north of San Francisco, also barred all movement of nuclear weapons and materials through the city as well as banning the conducting of nuclear research (none of which the town had ever been involved in). When the proposed ordinance went to the full council, the only change made, it seems, was to reduce the potential fine to $500.

THE MAYOR OF SPRINGFIELD, Illinois, suffered a heart attack in 1981 during a council meeting. The council voted 19–18 to wish him an early recovery.

TOWN COUNCILORS IN RAJNEESHPURAM, a community of 500 in Oregon, passed a resolution in 1982 making joke-telling obligatory at every council meeting. At least one councilor had to tell a joke at the start and end of each meeting. Officials said the aim was to make humor an integral part of council business.

HANOVER, GERMANY, CITY COUNCIL released an advent calendar for Christmas 2007 intended to portray all aspects of the city's culture—literally. Amid the singing children and Santa Claus distributing presents, the windows also revealed a depiction of the city's most notorious serial killer, Fritz Haarmann, hiding behind a tree with a meat cleaver in hand. Haarmann was executed in 1925 for the murder of 24 people, whose bodies he dismembered and sold as meat on the local black market. The tourist board defended the inclusion, saying the killer was "part of our city's history."

UK COUNCILORS ON THE South Lakeland Council in the Lake District took time to reorganize themselves in November 1976. The changes included the Tourism, Recreation, and Amenities Department becoming the Amenities, Recreation, and Tourism Department.

COMMISSIONERS IN MANATEE COUNTY, south of Tampa, Florida, decided to pass a local ordinance in April 1999 to raise local community dress standards. They ruled that women in the county were banned from exposing more than 75 percent of their breasts, and both sexes were banned from revealing more than two-thirds of their buttocks. Sheriff's Office spokesperson Dave Bristow told puzzled newsmen that the law enforcement agencies needed time to work out how to implement the law. "I don't think we'll be tape-measuring," he said.

THEY COULD CONSULT THE local ordinance passed in 1996 by legislators in St. John's County, Florida, when they sought to ban nude dancing. The law required that one-third of a dancer's buttocks be covered. It then described in fine detail how this was to be calculated. The description, for legal purposes, of "buttocks" ran to 328 words.

COUNCILORS IN KLEBERG COUNTY, Texas, outlawed the use of the greeting "hello" in 1997 and unanimously decreed that county officials should respond to telephone calls with "heaven-o" instead. The official resolution passed cited the "negative" connotations of "hello," as it contained the word "hell." In contrast, "heaven-o" is "a symbol of peace, friendship, and welcome" in this "age of anxiety."

In 2000, THE FOUR members of Gretna city council in Louisiana considered the weighty issue of whether it was legal to throw panties at carnival floats during the town's Mardi Gras celebrations. In a 4–0 vote, it unanimously endorsed proponents of the practice, who had maintained it was a long-running tradition of the event. Councilors did take time to differentiate on "throws," ruling that it would be illegal to throw anything depicting "male or female genitalia, is lewd or lascivious, and includes, but is not limited to, condoms and inflatable paraphernalia."

In 1981, WIGAN COUNCIL in England told Harry and Esther Hough, who had successfully fostered 47 children, that they were not fit to adopt because their marriage was too happy, and that children placed with them would not be sufficiently exposed to "negative experiences." In a letter to the couple, the area Social Services head David Wright told them, "It would seem that both of you have had few, if any, negative experiences when children yourselves, and also seem to enjoy a marital relationship where rows and arguments have no place." On those grounds, they were judged unsuited to bring up children long term.

THE BOROUGH COUNCIL IN Colne, Lancashire, put a kitten on its "dangerous animals" database in 2003 because it had scratched a building inspector. It also told homeowner Brian Jackson that as a result of the incident, which was formally registered as an "attack," his address would be blacklisted for all other council workers. When he appealed, Jackson managed to have his house delisted—but only on the technicality that the kitten was not his, but a neighbor's.

THE AUTHORITIES IN ST. Austell, Cornwall, put up the town's 2006 Christmas decorations in mid-September after it lost storage facilities for them. It was cheaper to install them early. While residents complained it made the town look "ridiculous," a spokesperson for the town looked on the bright side: "They're not doing anyone any harm. It saves a job later when the weather is more inclement."

SOUTH GLOUCESTERSHIRE COUNCIL WAS three weeks away from completing its $3,201,940 public library in Emersons Green, north Bristol, in March 2003 when it realized that no one had ordered—or budgeted for—any books for the new establishment. The council had to postpone the opening, and found itself needing to find another $376,228 to pay for the books, and for shelves to stack them on that had also been forgotten. Its official spokesperson blamed the mistake on the council being "a large organization. We won't get things right a hundred percent of the time."

 BRISTOL CITY COUNCIL LAUNCHED a "Don't Use a Padlock" initiative in 2008 that asked allotment holders not to lock their council-owned sheds so that thieves did not force their way into property and damage it. The aim was to save money because fewer sheds would need repairing after burglaries. A council spokesperson said that "where sheds have been repeatedly broken into, our advice is not to padlock them as forced entry often results in the doors being jemmied off." He did acknowledge that the guidance offered little protection for gardeners' equipment stored inside the sheds. The initiative foundered when Avon and Somerset Police directly contradicted the scheme by telling shed owners to securely lock their premises.

COUNCILORS ON BLACKPOOL COUNCIL devoted debating time in March 2008 to deciding to lift a ban on the Rolling Stones performing in the town that had been imposed 44 years earlier following a riot. It was not clear what had motivated the council to reconsider its stance after so long a time, but council leader Peter Callow proudly told press that they were writing to the group and that "they are welcome to play here again."

THE NAME GAME

Town councilors in Avon, Colorado, held a public contest in 1992 to name a new bridge over the Eagle River, which runs through the town. After sifting through 84 proposals, they rejected suggestions such as "Eagle Crossing" and chose as its official name, "Bob." It is still so named to this day.

TOWN LEADERS IN ISMAY, Montana (population 19, the smallest town in the state), were persuaded by a Kansas radio station in 1993 to rename their hamlet "Joe" in honor of Joe Montana, the celebrated American football star who had just arrived at the Kansas City Chiefs. For a year, the town basked in local fame as Joe, Montana. Although it soon lapsed back to calling itself lsmay, as late as 2002 the old signs were still proclaiming the adopted name.

THE TOWN COUNCILORS OF Halfway, Oregon, a tiny settlement of 362 people in the east of the state near the Idaho border, agreed in January 2000 to rename their community Half.com in a commercial tie-in with a newly launched secondhand goods Internet site based in Philadelphia. In exchange for $100,000, 20 free computers and the prospect of tourist fame, Mayor Dick Crow promoted his town as the world's first "dot-com" city. "It'll put our name on the map. By changing our name to Half.com, our community can greatly benefit from the success of the Internet." In fact, the town saw little change. By contrast, the owners of Half.com the company sold out to eBay later in the same year for a staggering $350 million.

IN NOVEMBER 2005, THE two town councilors of Clark, Texas (population 218), agreed unanimously to accept a challenge from Echostar Communications, the second-largest satellite TV company in the United States, that promised 10 years of free TV service to any town that agreed to rename itself after the company's Dish Network brand. The town had to agree to change its name legally and permanently, and on all government buildings, official letterheads, and road signs. In return, every single residence would be equipped with a reception dish free of charge. So Clark became DISH, Texas. This move was probably only made possible by the fact that the mayor responsible for leading the change had defeated the town's founder and namesake L. E. Clark only months earlier.

As the PR stunt had been budgeted to cost the company $4 million per thousand households, the fact that there were a mere 55 residences in the township gave the company reason to be content on its side too. The rural outpost north of Dallas hoped to attract growth by the move.

ON THE ROADS

Dave Heilmann, mayor of Oak Lawn, a suburb of Chicago, introduced an unorthodox traffic-calming measure in the middle of 2007 by winning the town council's approval for adding nonstandard warning messages to stop signs at more than 50 junctions around the area. Designed to catch the attention of drivers, residents were invited to submit their ideas. Among those that got erected directly underneath the octagonal stop boards were "In the Naaaame of Love," "Whoa, Whoa, Wait a Minute," "Billion Dollar Fine," "And Smell the Roses," and "Means You Aren't Moving." After concerns were raised by the Federal Highway Administration and the Illinois Transportation Department, the council was forced to take them down in April 2008 under threat of losing infrastructure funding.

THE DANISH ROAD SAFETY Council attracted global attention and opprobrium in equal measure in 2006 for its speed reduction campaign, which comprised a video of topless models standing by the roadside waving 50 kph speed limit signs and jiggling their breasts at drivers. It became a hit on the Internet and a spokesperson for the council reported it had had a "very positive reaction" for drawing attention to the problem of speeding drivers in Denmark. She claimed feedback showed that half of drivers would think more about the dangers of speeding.

COUNCILORS IN THE SMALL Dutch town of Culemborg, 10 miles south of Utrecht, introduced a controversial traffic-calming scheme in September 1996—sheep. Initially, six were let loose in the town to wander at will through the busy roads, leaving it to drivers to slow down to avoid hitting them. There were plans for up to a hundred to be released if the experiment proved successful. Animal welfare groups declared themselves outraged at the project.

THE HIGHWAYS AUTHORITY MANAGING the stretch of the A40(M) Westway in west London removed all street lighting in 2007. Signs were erected along the entire route pronouncing "no street lighting." Users of the road pointed out the futility of the investment: in daytime the signs were of no value; at night, they could not be seen by drivers because of the lack of street lighting.

AFTER THE SEVERE WINTER of 2010 left nearly half the roads across Germany damaged by potholes, the council in the eastern village of Niederzimmern tackled the problem by a scheme that enabled residents to meet the cost of an individual hole repair and have a personalized message placed on the finished smooth surface. For $66, the council would fill in a designated pothole and leave whatever message the "owner" of the hole wanted. A number of businesses were reported to have bought up holes as cheap advertising space.

TAX DOLLARS

After a survey in 1991 revealed that local taxpayers were unhappy at the state of pavements and roads, Birmingham city council commissioned a further study, costing $9,600, to find out what people thought of potholes. The city engineer defended the decision to spend the money this way rather than mend some holes: "It is essential that in-depth views of the public be obtained to provide detailed understanding of dissatisfaction."

BASSINGBOURN PARISH COUNCIL IN Cambridgeshire voted in March 2005 to put $8,000 toward a bronze sculpture of a pile of dinosaur dung to commemorate the locality's wealth, which was created in the nineteenth century by mining fossilized dung for fertilizer. South Cambridgeshire District Council had agreed to fund the other half of the $16,000 that the memorial would cost.

FYLDE BOROUGH COUNCIL, IN Lancashire, spent $24,000 in 2006 on a "risk assessment study" of kite flying on local beaches after a single incident when a walker became entangled in a flyer's lines.

TO THE BEMUSEMENT OF local taxpayers, Cambridgeshire County Council decided in January 2006 to undertake a costly consultation exercise with residents on the subject of how it should undertake consultation exercises with residents. The council's plans for traffic-calming measures would be consulted on once the council felt it was satisfied it knew the way people preferred to be consulted. The chair of the committee responsible for all this said she hoped the consultation on consultations exercise would "improve communications" between the council and the public.

JETTISONING THE EVOCATIVE TOURIST slogan of its predecessor government ("The Best Small Country in the World"), the first ever Scottish Nationalist administration spent $200,000 when it came to power in 2007 on a consultancy with a top advertising agency to develop a new branding to match the new era. Six months, and much anticipation, later the new tag line was unveiled in November: "Welcome to Scotland."

EAST HERTS COUNCIL SPENT $320 to get a consultant to write a 17-page report on how staff should safely make a cup of tea after the server at the council's headquarters in Bishop's Stortford was let go in 2006.

TWO COUNCILS IN LANCASHIRE spent $3,500 in 2008 on a 10-minute DVD demonstrating to ratepayers how they should put rubbish in their bins. Using actors carting wheeled bins to the front of houses and sorting through items, the film for Fylde and Wyre councils was designed to help distinguish between various recycling schemes. It portrayed a man helping a women to identify a cardboard cereal box that should be placed in the paper-recycle carton, and told viewers that pieces of wood such as a twig could be classified as garden waste, whereas larger pieces ("like a door frame") could not. "It's a complete waste of money," campaigners against bureaucratic waste complained.

The film was distributed to householders throughout the two councils' areas. It did not go unnoticed that DVDs were one of the most difficult items to recycle. They were probably likely to be heading only for the landfill.

SMALL TOWN MISHAPS

Swansea city council incurred ridicule in 2008 for failing to spot a wrong translation on a bilingual English-Welsh road sign that it erected in the town to bar entry for trucks to a residential area. The Welsh translation was somewhat more prosaic. Emailing the text ("No entry for heavy goods vehicles. Residential site only") to its in-house translation service, the evidently non-Welsh speaker had taken down the reply received, which was passed on to the manufacturers, who clearly were less than proficient Welsh speakers too. What resulted was the emblazoning on the sign of the translator's out-of-office notifier ("I am not in the office at the moment. Please send any work to be translated").

Despite the blanket policy for translating road signs throughout the principality, in Swansea the Welsh language is actually used by only 12 percent of the population.

BIRMINGHAM, ENGLAND, CITY COUNCIL printed and distributed 360,000 leaflets in August 2008 updating local taxpayers on the city's progress on recycling. Under a banner headline "Thank You, Birmingham" lay a picture of a smart and modernistic city skyline that residents quickly spotted did not look like their Birmingham. It wasn't. For unexplained reasons the picture was of Birmingham, Alabama. The council initially claimed it was meant to represent a "generic skyline." Suspicions fell on it more likely being the unchecked work of a less-than-geographically astute trainee: a Google search on the Internet for "Birmingham" produced exactly the same photograph.

FORESTRY COMMISSION OFFICIALS GOT bad press in 1984 when a luncheon hosted by chair Sir David Montgomery during a seminar on wildlife conservation was revealed to include venison and squirrel pie.

THE EAST ESSEX HEALTH Authority launched a "Better Health" campaign in 1986 using an expensively designed logo featuring a cardiogram. Only at the last minute did a doctor spot that the cardiogram showed that the patient would be dead.

A $1 MILLION FIRE station in Charleston, West Virginia, could not open when building work finished in January 2000, as the city authority that commissioned it discovered that it failed to comply with its own fire regulations.

ROCHDALE BOROUGH COUNCIL'S NEW computerized planning application system thwarted a resident's attempt to lodge an objection to his neighbor's plans because the software blocked all his email messages, as they contained the word "erection." Ray Kennedy tried three times to send his complaint. The last one arrived after the application had been approved.

BASILDON COUNCIL HAD TO change the color of 150 dog litter bins in 2000 from red to grey after residents began posting letters in them thinking they were mailboxes.

CHELTENHAM TOWN COUNCIL INTRODUCED a scheme in the spring of 2007 to highlight the problem of dog owners who fail to clean up after their pets. Its dog wardens began to circle each pile of dog droppings with spray paint, apparently in an attempt to shame walkers into coming back to do the honorable thing. A warden even returned a week later to paint a fresh color around the offending pile if it was still there to embarrass offenders further. According to Rob Garnham, the councilor responsible for the local environment, "It has the effect of allowing us to...identify if this is an ongoing problem." Residents, however, pointed out the less than aesthetic effect for the genteel spa town of creating multiple brightly colored circles on footpaths across the community spotlighting the mess. One resident observed, "Some of the pavements look like a weird dirty protest in the Tate Gallery."

FROM THE HISTORY BOOKS

Mayors have sometimes shown an unwillingness to be confined to local matters or, in some cases, even earthly ones. During a UFO "flap" in October 1954 that saw dozens of reports of unidentified flying objects over southeastern France, Lucien Lejeune, mayor of Chateauneuf-du-Pape, issued a formal decree prohibiting "the overflight, the landing, and the takeoff of aircraft known as flying saucers" anywhere within his community. It also threatened that any landing in breach of the decree would end with the occupants being put in jail "immediately." The edict was to be enforced by a single rural police officer assisted by the local forest keeper. Of particular note was the added information that the announcement had even been sent to, and approved by, the Département's Prefect, the next most senior official in the region.

TIMES CHANGE. BY 1976, the mayor of another southern French town, this time in the southwest, declared his community to be the world's first UFO-port, welcoming landings by any visitor from outer space. On August 15, the mayor of Ares, near Bordeaux, along with all his village councilors and an air force officer, formally inaugurated the landing strip. The mayor gave the rationale for the opening: "The reason that flying saucers have never landed on Earth is because there are no airports for them." He promised the UFO-port would remain open 24 hours a day, and offered a special bonus for the first arrival—it would be exempted from landing fees. Nearly four decades on, it has still to receive any business.

SMALL COMMUNITIES HAVE MARKED critical moments in their development in equally bizarre ways. The local council of the cotton-growing town of Enterprise, Alabama, erected a monument to the industry's principal enemy, the boll weevil, in 1919. It is the world's only monument built to honor an agricultural pest. They did so because the devastation of the local cotton plantations by the bug forced the community to diversify its economy, which in the long run ensured the future of the town. The plaque on the statue of a woman holding aloft a huge weevil foresightedly dedicates it "in profound appreciation of the Boll Weevil and what it has done as the herald of prosperity."

9

PARTING THOUGHTS

We have witnessed the extremes that politics can produce. Actions, they say, speak louder than words. But the motivations of politicians can be just as entertaining and thought provoking. To round off our collection of political foolishness, we leave some parting thoughts.

POLITICS OBSERVED

Politics is derived from two words—"poly" meaning many and "tics" meaning small, blood-sucking insects.

(Anon)

Political promises go in one year and out the other.

(Anon)

Politics is the skilled use of blunt objects.

Lester Pearson, Canadian prime minister

Never mistake motion for action.

Ernest Hemingway

Man's capacity for justice makes democracy possible; man's inclination for injustice makes democracy necessary.

Reinhold Niebuhr, The Children of Light and the Children of Darkness

Ninety percent of politicians give the other 10 percent a bad name.

Henry Kissinger, former
U.S. national security advisor
and secretary of state, 1978

THE CIVIL SERVICE

It's like watching an elephant get pregnant. Everything's done on a very high level, there's a lot of commotion, and it takes 22 months for anything to happen.

U.S. President Franklin Roosevelt,
on working with the State Department

The only thing that saves us from bureaucracy is its inefficiency. An efficient bureaucracy is the greatest threat to freedom.

Eugene McCarthy, U.S. politician, 1979

The single most exciting thing you encounter in government is competence, because it's so rare.

Daniel Moynihan, U.S. senator, 1976

POLITICAL PERSPECTIVES

I ask you to judge me by the enemies I have made.

Franklin D. Roosevelt

The secret is to always let the other man have your way.

Claiborne Pell, U.S. senator, 1987

He's a great ex-president. It's a shame he couldn't have gone directly to the ex-presidency.

Thomas Mann, Brookings Institute,
on ex-President Jimmy Carter's success
in mediating with North Korea, 1994

POLITICAL LIFE

The main advantage of being famous is that when you bore
people at dinner parties they think it is their fault.

Henry Kissinger

Chief Secretary, I'm afraid there is no money. Kind regards
and good luck.

Outgoing second-in-command of the Treasury,
Liam Byrne, leaving a message for his successor,
David Laws, after the British general election, 2010

One thing about a pig. He thinks he's warm if his nose
is warm. I saw a bunch of pigs one time that had frozen
together in a circle, each one's nose tucked under the rump
of the one in front. We have a lot of pigs in politics.

Eugene McCarthy, U.S. politician, 1968

I was at a big international conference, when a woman who seemed vaguely familiar asked me where I was from. "I'm Tony Blair from the British Labor Party," I replied. "And you are?" "My name is Beatrice and I'm from the Netherlands." "Beatrice who?" "Just Beatrice." "What do you do?" I asked. "I am the queen."

> *Prime Minister Tony Blair, in a 1999 interview to* Woman's Journal, *revealing his worst social gaffe.*

Jack Straw, British home secretary, visiting a retirement home in 1999, introduced himself to a resident with the greeting, "Do you know who I am?" The elderly woman replied, "No, dear, but if you ask matron, she will tell you." Keep your sense of humor about your position. The higher a monkey climbs, the more you see his behind.

> *Donald Rumsfeld, U.S. defense secretary,*
> *on serving President Ford 1974–76*

I would never do anything to deride the profession of politics—although I think it is a form of madness.

> *Lord Home, former prime minister, 1983*

It is in the national interest for me to take an afternoon nap because I cannot initiate anything while I am asleep.

Calvin Coolidge, U.S. president 1923–29

If you've got 'em by the balls, their hearts and minds will follow.

Sign on desk of Charles "Chuck" Colson,
special counsel to Richard Nixon, 1969–73

ELECTIONS

It's not who votes that counts, but who counts the votes.

Anonymous graffiti, 1980s

Trust is not having to guess what a candidate means.

Gerald Ford, U.S. president, 1976

Be thankful only one of them can win.

Bumper sticker, Nixon-Kennedy contest, 1960

In your heart, you know he's right.

Campaign slogan, right-wing Republican
candidate Barry Goldwater, 1964